D1515827

LOVE WORK,
LIVE LIFE!

LOVE WORK, LIVE LIFE!

Releasing God's Purpose in Work

David Oliver

Authentic

Copyright © 2006 David Oliver

12 11 10 09 08 07 06   7 6 5 4 3 2 1

First Published in 2006 by Authentic Media
9 Holdom Avenue, Bletchley, Milton Keynes, Bucks, MK1 1QR
and 129 Mobilization Drive, Waynesboro, GA 30830-4575, USA
www.authenticmedia.co.uk
Authentic Media is a division of Send the Light Ltd. (registered charity no. 270162).

Parts of this book have been previously published as *Work: Prison or Place of Destiny?*
First published in 1999 by Word Publishing.

The right of David Oliver to be identified as the author of this work has been asserted
by him in accordance with the Copyright, Designs and Patents Act 1988.

All rights reserved. No part of this publication may be reproduced, stored in a retrieval
system, or transmitted in any form or by any means, electronic, mechanical, photocopy-
ing, recording or otherwise, without the prior permission of the publisher or a licence
permitting restricted copying. In the UK such licences are issued by the Copyright
Licensing Agency, 90 Tottenham Court Road,
London, W1P 9HE.

British Library Cataloguing in Publication Data

A catalogue record for this book is available from
the British Library.

ISBN 1-86024-529-3

Unless otherwise indicated, all scripture quotations are from the NEW KING JAMES
VERSION © 1979, 1980, 1982 Thomas Nelson, Inc. All rights reserved.
Scripture quotations marked NIV are from the
HOLY BIBLE NEW INTERNATIONAL VERSION © 1973, 1978, 1984
by the International Bible Society. Used by permission of
Hodder & Stoughton Ltd. All rights reserved.

Cover design by Allison Hodgkiss, Care for the Family
Print Management by Adare Carwin
Printed in Great Britain by J.H. Haynes and Co., Sparkford

Contents

Foreword

I can't tell you how often I have had conversations with people who believed they would be more obedient to God and more fulfilled in their lives if they left their 'ordinary job' and entered 'full-time Christian service'. I remember one man who had already made that decision telling me he couldn't wait to begin his new job working for a Christian ministry as he was 'tired of office politics'. I didn't have the heart to disillusion him.

It's easy to see how we can embrace that mindset. We might regard work as a result of the Fall – a symptom of living in a world that's far away from God. And, let's be honest, sometimes at our desk, on our shift or on the road, we can feel a very long way away from God. We might even go to work every day hoping that today's the day that he will call us to work 'full-time' for him.

But David Oliver urges us to realise that there is an eternal value in what we are doing right now. Our job might not seem as if it directly benefits people, but the way we work impacts many – not least those we work with.

It's not hard to lose sight of that and come to believe that the place where we spend most of our week is somehow outside of God's plan for our lives. That's why I'm delighted that David has written this book. Like him, I'm hoping that thousands of us will rediscover the truth that God wants to use us in our daily work – and that, in fact, we are working for him regardless of who signs our pay cheques.

It can be hard in the world of work, but it's harder by far if we choose to go to work alone. My hope is that David's message will encourage all of us to see that wherever we go, God goes with us. Even at 9 a.m. on a Monday morning.

Rob Parsons
Executive Director, Care for the Family

To My Family

You are a hard-working family and I love you. It is very special to me to see my wife and children hard at work in some chosen sphere or other. That is probably one of the most meaningful things that I could experience. Thank you each of you for seeing the value of work and giving yourselves to it.

Thank you, too, for often releasing me into the call of work when it takes me places. And thank you for catching the Spirit's vision and beginning to fly with it for yourselves.

Waking Up to Work

Some years ago, my wife, Gill, and I had the children looked after while we travelled to Bognor Regis and borrowed her parents' static caravan for the weekend. We were into weekends away, but this one was going to be completely different. No romantic meals for two. No trips out. So, what were we doing there? – Listening to hours of material about the kingdom of God! We didn't want to leave until we had allowed that teaching to change our lives – and change they did!

Even back then, I had been preaching about the place of work in Christian life, having been inspired by a number of leading thinkers. However, my wife and I remained frustrated by the reality that the majority of churches and their leaders seemed more or less apathetic when it came to preaching and teaching about work, despite its obvious importance to vast numbers of people they had pastoral responsibility for.

What a difference a few years can make! When I first wrote about Christians and work back in 1999, there were only two other books that I knew of on the same subject matter. As I write this in 2005 there are over forty books published in the UK on the subject. Spring Harvest regularly include workplace issues in their main events as well as producing a number of dedicated seminars. Personally speaking, I have been invited time and again to talk about 'The kingdom of God and work' in the UK, Kenya, Sweden, Zimbabwe, the USA, India and Singapore. I have even been invited for the first time ever by a Bible college, to broach this subject. Work has always been on God's agenda – it would appear that finally it is on the agenda of the church!

So, what was it that so dramatically changed our lives during that long weekend in Bognor? Gill and I had always assumed we had the 'magical-call' to 'full-time' ministry. Various events had led us towards what we thought was our calling. We were travelling all over the place preaching and teaching. Our understanding was that full-time ministry was working for and into the church. But that weekend and the days that followed really opened our eyes. A new horizon opened up, the possibility that our ministry could be shared equally between the world of work and the world of the church. More importantly, we came to realise the truth that our work and our calling were a seamless whole. God did not divide life into unconnected compartments labelled 'Work' and 'Church'.

I understand the pressures of work on the shop floor, I understand the tremendous privileges of being employed and the many frustrations that it can bring. I know what it is to run a company with all the blessings and tensions involved. But more than all of the above, I believe that the workplace is the primary arena in which the kingdom of God can actually touch our lives and the lives of those we work with.

Whatever you are doing in life, whether you are in church-paid ministry, in education, the caring professions, whether you're a public servant, run your own business of some other kind, stay-at-home to look after your children or care for other people's; work on the shop floor or as a volunteer – may God bless you, because you are doing the work of building the kingdom.

Love Work as a Place of Destiny

1.

Work: Prison or Destiny?

(It depends on what you believe)

Before we go any further, ask yourself these questions:

- What do you think about work?
- What does God think about it?
- What does the Bible teach about it?

The answers you give to these questions are of vital importance, for what you believe will determine whether you view work as a place of destiny where you can live out fully your Christian life, or a prison, preventing you from getting on with your 'real' work of worshipping and serving God.

All quiet on the working front

When I preach or teach about work, I will often ask the audience, 'How many of you have ever heard a sermon on work?' In nearly every case, it is less than 50 per cent. Until a few years ago, close to 100 per cent of Christians said that they had never heard a single sermon about work! Not only that, 75 per cent have never been asked about how their work relates to their Christian faith by those pastorally responsible for them.

These are still startling statistics. What they tell us is that Christians are not being equipped for the place where they spend 65 per cent of their time. Worse than that, there is an implicit message being sent out by the church that what we spend most of our lives doing is irrelevant to our faith and undervalued by God. Is there any wonder so many Christians struggle at work.

Is work a hindrance to faith, or the one place in reality where I can most fully express my Christianity? Is work minimising my opportunity to serve God or is it a wonderful, challenging, fulfilling and God-given environment? Clearly these are important and challenging questions we need to be asking.

It depends on what you believe!

What do we mean by work? It means the obvious things, like one's paid employment. It also includes housework, DIY maintenance on your home, studying at college or university, helping with the homework. Work is work, whether it is paid or not. The real question, however, is this: *Do we think that the work we do (full- or part-time, paid or voluntary) is Christian work, a 'ministry' worthy of the kingdom of God?*

There can be a real danger in what we believe. That danger is to have a mindset that thinks primarily about Christian work as that which happens on a Sunday, or serves the Christian community in some way (leading a home group, singing in the worship group, stewarding on a Sunday, teaching in Sunday School, running the youth club, etc), and the rest of our labour as simply 'work'.

It's not hard to see how thousands of Christians have ended up with this dichotomy. For most of us, our leaders, our pastors and ministers, those who mentor and disciple us will almost certainly be in 'full-time' Christian work. The problem is, God-given as all those ministries are – and thank God for them – this can easily leave us with a twisted or distorted view about Christians and work. For instance, I may come to believe that I am only fully approved and valued by God, or recognised by the church, when my God-given gifts are expressed within a church context. Perhaps more insidious is the thought that I could be more pleasing to God, more effective as a person, and more valuable as an individual, if I were working more in the church, or for the church. Nothing could be further from the truth.

I remember one of my friends, Niall Barry, said to me one day, 'You know you have his permission to be successful; you have his blessing to be successful.' I was, and am, so grateful for those words, but what an indictment that they should ever be necessary. I have met thousands of men and women who somehow feel less than spiritual, even guilty, because they are working day after day in a non-church environment. I have met many who can't really enjoy it because of various beliefs and pressures. I have met others who are so restless, so dissatisfied, so frustrated because they can't see a way out of the prison of work. I want the words of my friend to be words of comfort and challenge. Could you dare to believe that when you go to work you are fulfilling a destiny written into the software of your life from heaven's programming department? Could you dare to believe this is what you were created for? If you could believe that, what difference would it make? Destiny! Just about every Christian you speak to is looking for the thing that God has apprehended them for. Suppose this is it? Yes, you and your job with your customers, your machines, your patients.

Working for God

When we look closely at the biblical stories of those who served God and his kingdom, few had 'full-time' ministries, as we would understand such an idea. Abraham is the father of the faith for both Jews and Gentiles. You don't get much more spiritual or significant than that. But he accomplished that role as a travelling farmer, a businessman, a landowner, a cattle rancher and an investor in silver and gold. Every tribe, tongue, and nation will one day stand before the throne of God; every tribe and tongue on the planet, and it will be because of God's promise to a working man. Rather than give up his work, he simply changed his working practice and his way of life to accommodate God's call. Moses was at different times an academic and a nomadic farmer. Jesus refers to the first prophet as Abel. But Abel was also one of Scripture's first recorded working men, and it was his work-based worship that brought pleasure to the creator. Joseph's prophetic ministry began in animal husbandry, took him into service in military households, prison management, and finally into the highest government office. Daniel's great visions came as he worked in the civil service and the king's court, heading up what was essentially a think tank, developing government policy and providing counsel. David was shepherd, poet, musician, military strategist and eventually a hard-working monarch.

What about the prophets? Amos ran a flock and a sycamore fig grove. Isaiah was in the king's court. Zephaniah was a socialite in court service, with political interest. Ezekiel, whilst coming from a priestly family, was incredibly well-versed in international affairs, culture, shipbuilding and literature. Nehemiah was a civil-service governor. Obadiah was head of palace management. Elisha was a wealthy landowner with the equivalent of twelve combine-harvesters.

And what about Jesus, the one we are called to follow? Well he was 'the carpenter' (Mark 6:3). As such, he would have been apprenticed, the senior partner in the family carpentry business. He would almost certainly have dealt with cash flow, pricing, quality, delivery and purchasing. His life, from the age of 12 to 30, was probably spent working as a tradesman. Jesus knew what it was to work on the shop floor! Compare that with the three years he spent on the road teaching and preaching. That's a ratio of 6:1. Even then Jesus spent the majority of his time with ordinary working people. He spoke with and ministered to those in the market place, with farmers and fishermen, carpenters and builders, tax-collectors and entrepreneurs, with servants and soldiers with housewives and lawyers. Indeed, he spent far more time ministering among the working population than he did in a place of worship. He even based his parables and stories about the kingdom of God on the ordinary working lives of those he encountered – sowers and vineyard workers, harvesters, house-builders, women sweeping the house, bankers, the armed forces.

If I were to ask you who were the key figures in the book of Acts in spreading the gospel, who would you suggest? Peter? Paul? What if I were to say that the key figures included two people in manufacturing, one in the armed forces and a high-end fashion dealer? Far fetched? Not really.

Priscilla and Aquilla were tent manufacturers. Paul met them in Athens and they worked together. The church at Corinth was born out of the teamwork that ensued and probably met in their home. Their manufacturing business was also the base from which Paul and the team operated and Paul was keen for it to be known wherever he went that he worked for his own living as a tentmaker. After travelling with Paul, Priscilla and Aquilla stayed in Ephesus. All the churches of the Gentiles were recorded as being grateful for them.

Cornelius was one of the first, but certainly not the last Roman soldier to be converted. These conversions of Roman soldiers were a strategic element, not only in spreading the gospel to the Gentiles, but also throughout the Roman Empire and into Europe.

The high-end fashion dealer was Lydia, who traded purple dye – an exclusive product in her day. She was the first European convert and her network almost certainly sparked the first church in Europe. She provided a home for Paul and his team – the first base for the first outreach team into Europe!

The point I'm trying to make in all this is that the Bible is full of examples of God at work through ordinary men and women. More than that, the Bible is a book about men and women at work, often written by men and women at work and written for men and women at work. Indeed, in Hebrews 11, which is the chapter on the heroes of the faith, at least fifteen people out of the seventeen mentioned were working men and women. That should inspire us, liberate us and encourage us. It means we can have faith and confidence that whatever work we are involved in, we are working for God.

God works

It's good to know that working men and women are at the centre of the Bible. But perhaps the most encouraging, value-giving and affirming revelation of all is that God works! The very first verse in the Bible says, 'In the beginning God created (*worked at*) the heavens and the earth' (addition mine). God is recorded as one who '*makes, forms, builds* and *plants*'. These are all words used elsewhere in Scripture to describe work. Then, in Genesis 2:3, 'God blessed the seventh day and made it holy, because on it he rested from all the work of creating that he had done (NIV).'

Whilst God's work can be distinguished from our own by the fact that he is all-powerful and his work is perfect, his work did involve many of the functions we consider work to be:

- he makes things – as a craftsman might;
- he categorises and names things – as a scientist might;
- he plans carefully – one process following another;
- he examines the quality of his work – quality control;
- he clearly defines each component's function – as an engineer might;
- he clearly defines humanity's role and provides resources – as a good manager might;
- his work reflects who he is – as we would like ours to do;
- he takes pleasure in his work – a job well done; satisfied.

Right through the Bible, God is represented as constantly working – ordering circumstances to change our lives, involving himself with nations and individuals. God is at work – ruling, delegating and providing. Philippians 2:13 says, 'for it is God who works in you both to will and to do for his good pleasure.' Both his will and his work are his good pleasure.

This is all positive stuff. But doesn't all we have learned so far leave us with an inevitable and appropriate question: With all this evidence and with all these examples, how come there is such an indifference or lack of active engagement in so many of God's people towards the world of work?

2.

The Big Lie

One of the biggest problems I face in communicating to Christians how important and valued the work they do is by God, is overcoming the pervasive heresy that work is worldly or secular and that church work is spiritual or sacred. Somehow, what amounts to a big lie, has crept into our thinking about work and faith with hardly anybody noticing or challenging this error. And yet, there is no such distinction anywhere in Scripture. In fact, the word 'secular' never appears in the Bible – not once!

From the very first chapter in the Bible, we get the clearest indication that spiritual activity and work are synonymous. In Genesis 1:2 ('the Spirit of God was hovering over the face of the waters'), God was working, and working by the Holy Spirit. Work was also the first responsibility given to humankind. Before God gave Adam his wife and family, he gave him work. The Lord took Adam and put him into the garden to work and take care of it. Adam was never placed on the planet to worship. He was placed here to work. Eve, too, was created and presented, because no helper was found, as Adam began the process of work. Work is not the result of the fall. Work was there before the fall, part of God's personality and integral to his faultless design. The fall simply tainted our God-given labour. From the very beginning men and women were created to have fellowship with each other, and with God, by working on his planet, serving each other and serving God in the process.

In Exodus 35, we see one of the first records of God choosing men and putting his Holy Spirit on them. What for? To act as priests or worship leaders? No! In verses 31–35 (NIV), talking about a man named Bezalel, it says:

> . . . he has filled him with the Spirit of God, with skill, ability and
> knowledge in all kinds of crafts . . . And he has given both him and
> Oholiab . . . the ability to teach others. He has filled them with skill
> to do all kinds of work . . .

Interesting isn't it that the first story of the Holy Spirit on
God's people has to do with art, design, manufacturing and
teaching.

The thought of work evokes poetry from the very heart of God.
In Psalm 104, the psalmist describes the wonders of creation in
poetry set to music. One of these wonders of creation is expressed
in verse 23, where it says, 'Man goes out to his work and to his
labour until the evening.'

God made us in his image so that we can fulfil his purpose in
ourselves and in the world by working. God in his providence
has placed each person to do the work of that place. There is
glory in our work – whatever work it may be. As William Tyndale
once wrote, 'There is no work better than another to please God;
to pour water, to wash dishes, to be a cobbler, or an apostle, all is
one; to wash dishes or to preach is all one as touching the deed,
to please God.'

I remember once, when I was working with YWAM, Corrie
Ten-Boom came up to me as I was washing dishes and simply
said, 'Young man, I would far rather be doing what you are doing
than what I do.' She had picked up my frustration with dish-
washing instead of preaching, and she was inserting into my life
a one sentence, theological foundation about God's attitude to
the work we do.

George Macdonald put it this way:

> If the soul of the believer be the temple of the Holy Spirit, then is
> not the place of that man's labour – his shop, his bank, his labora-
> tory, his school, his factory – the temple of Jesus Christ where the
> spirit of man is at work?

I often wondered why it was so difficult to convince successful
businessmen of their need of God. I've finally come to the con-
clusion that work is so spiritual, so God-like, that it virtually fills
the spiritual vacuum in the lives of people who give themselves

to it. Ironic evidence perhaps, that work is spiritual, deeply spiritual.

It was all Greek to me!

My life is full of both church work and business consultancy. I train people, run seminars and provide strategic and marketing consultancy. I also travel the world preaching. Sometimes the two dimensions seem to pull each other apart.

I used to have a regular moan at God about this. Sometimes I used to pray like this: 'Lord, can't you just let me be a preacher? I could be a great preacher.' Only to find myself a few days later praying, 'Lord, can't you just let me focus on business? If I were more focused, I could employ more people and make large sums of money for your kingdom.' It's a strange analogy, but I used to feel my life was like a letter 'Y' – starting off as a single, coherent, continuous line, but then suddenly dividing and veering off in opposite directions.

Imagine my surprise, therefore, when one day a preacher called Dennis Peacocke singled me out in a meeting and said, 'You see a Y, but it is not so, it is a single rod.' I was separating the two compartments – business/church, secular/sacred, consultancy/ministry. But God was saying as clearly as if he were in the room, 'It isn't like that, it is a single life flow.'

This sacred/secular divide isn't a new idea grown in the hustle and bustle of our modern, busy working lives. The idea that work is secular and not sacred is an ancient concept taught by Greek pagans that has slowly permeated church thinking and practice. It has disempowered men and women who otherwise would have been productive. It has prevented God's people from seeing the sacredness of work.

So as long as this great lie is perpetuated in our midst it will affect how we feel about ourselves, about the value of what we do, and give us a false perspective about the church. Full-time or any form of work in the church is not more spiritual. It is not more highly valued by God. The church is not the kingdom of God and nor is our work place, but both have a vital part to play bringing it about.

When we view work as secular it has profound implications. Why? Because it takes meaning, value and a sense of calling away from what we do. Call it secular long enough – which we have – and that is what it will become – which it has.

Work is our God-given destiny

It's important to understand that for most of us our destiny will not primarily be within the structures of church. This may cause enormous frustrations and tensions. We can't see our ultimate destiny or calling in the church infrastructure, and yet somehow we feel reluctant, guilty, carnal or even second best if we begin to consider options that extend beyond the church's sphere or realm.

I have heard it said, directly and by implication, that really-spiritual people will become 'full-time'. Our corrupted belief systems and some elements of church culture, have produced a generation of men and women who have a deep-seated conviction that to be called to 'full-time' ministry is what really matters. Over the years I have spoken to hundreds, probably thousands, who feel this way and who deep down believe this is their end or destiny, or who desperately hope that it is.

The irony of this way of thinking is that it can rob us of our destiny. It also robs our employer of a whole heart and commitment to our work. It can rob gifted entrepreneurs from releasing that gift for the kingdom of God. It produces in us a short term mentality towards work – deep down always hoping for, always longing for, the call to 'higher' more spiritual things.

But church is not a 'higher thing', or more spiritual, than the sphere of work in which we should be living out our destiny. Work, in whatever context, is the most spiritual thing you can ever do. Therefore, church should be a supportive family for the work we do. It needs to equip us and send us out into every sphere of service, work and activity and at the same time hold us accountable to the fact that God has called us to our work. It should value us for the work we do as God values us. For most of us, our destiny is not the gathered church; rather church is there to ensure that I fulfil my destiny wherever God has called me.

The church needs to equip us as individuals and send us out into every sphere of service, work and activity. Look at Ephesians 4:12 – 'for the equipping of the saints for the work of ministry'. We don't hold all the best to ourselves – we are to give our best freely.

This fact then prompts another self-evident question: Are you called or led by God to your place of work? It's surprising how few of us take the time to pray about this important question. After all, work occupies more than half of our waking hours. The other half is divided into family time (work on the house, garden, etc), church involvement, time alone with God and relaxation. We will spend more time working than we will in any one of those other areas. It is, therefore, of extreme weight and importance – 40 to 50 hours a week working, as against 20 hours at home and far fewer hours spent in church activities. Because of this, we need to check with God that we are not wasting the best part of each day, each week and each year doing something God never intended us to be doing. How many of us work just for the money rather than an act of godly service? Money makes a lousy master and as the Bible rightly suggests you can't serve God and Mammon.

To work is a God-given gift, but God wants all of us to have the right motivations, to use our gifts and talents and to serve him and other people by what we do. In this way we become part of God's activity in bringing the kingdom of God to those we work with and for. So please, take some time to pray and seek God about your work.

If we know that our work is the calling of God, then we can be assured that he will bless that work and help us to do our jobs to the best of our abilities. In work, my daily motive should be that God has called or led me here. This is where I will interface or introduce the kingdom of God. I work because I am called to it, God has placed me here, and it's my primary sphere to live out what it means to 'seek first the kingdom of God'.

It is time to settle the issue. Time is short and our lives are short. Why do I do what I do? Am I in it because it is easy? Am I in it because of the money it makes? Am I in it for myself, adding God to what I want to do? Or am I in it because I am confident it is where God has placed me for now? It is time to settle the fact that my work is not an accident, it is where God has called me and it is where he has placed me.

> Do we work because we are disciples and this is where God has led us? If that is our primary motivation above all the others, then we will bring pleasure to God and release his presence in our workplace.

I want to encourage us to find a place of faith – faith for our jobs and our businesses, faith for the projects for which we are responsible. I want to encourage us to see work as a high calling, to see it as valid and as valuable. I want us to have the peace and joy that come with knowing that we are in the centre of God's will – not just as a stop-gap. I want us to believe that God desires his Spirit in us to flow through our farms, our offices, our homes, our colleges and universities, our factories, our practices, our consultancies. Faith to believe that God can, and has, planned to use me in my work. Faith to believe that I am where he has called or led me. In short, faith to believe that our work is a place of destiny that can be a joy for ourselves and a pleasure to the heart of God.

3.

Working for the Kingdom

What do the words 'calling' and 'vocation' mean to you? What images do they conjure up? For many of us, sensing that God has called us to the work we do is vital to feeling needed and valued. So is the belief that what we have been called to is a vocation and not just any old job. But these words are the source of much confusion, heartache and disappointment among Christians. A common problem for Christians, one of the main reasons for ineffectiveness, is uncertainty about their calling to a job.

Calling is often associated with some sort of divine, supernatural encounter – a kind of commissioning recalled from our vivid recollections of Bible stories. Vocation is often used to describe an occupation that has at its heart service to people – medicine and education are the areas that most readily spring to mind. The problem with these ideas is that they reinforce the dualism or spiritual aristocracy that we have worked hard to dismantle in the book so far. In other words, only a few can have the spiritual type jobs and the vocational ones. Therefore, it will probably help if we clear up a couple of misconceptions.

1. *Are vocation and calling synonymous?* The word 'vocation' does not appear in Scripture; its dictionary definition can mean a specified profession or trade, or a special urge to a calling or career. It comes from the Latin word *vocare* – to call. So the two words are closely linked.

2. *What does the Bible have to say about calling?* Let me quote Os Guinness from *The Call*, 'Calling is the truth that God calls us to himself so decisively that everything we are, everything we do, and everything we have is invested with a special devotion and dynamism lived out as a response to his summons service.'

One call for us all

One of the main problems is that we have developed an unhealthy preoccupation with the idea of having a personal, specific individual call from God. But 'calling' in the New Testament doesn't have this narrow sense of personal destiny. The New Testament word for calling is *klesis* meaning invited, called or summoned. As a church we are *all* called out as one community – *Ekklesia*. Every Christian is called, no matter what they do. The good news of the gospel is that there is no favouritism, no elitism, no redundancy, no chance that we will be forgotten and no chance that we have been overlooked.

We are all called to serve both God and, through our work, those around us. There is no exception. Paul says 'whatever you do, do it heartily [with a whole-hearted approach], as to the Lord and not to men, knowing from the Lord you will receive the reward...' Jesus made it clear that we are to seek first the kingdom of God, right where we are, through whatever work we are doing at the moment. If we are constantly looking elsewhere, or waiting for that special call, then we run a very real danger that we will miss what God has for us today.

I remember talking with a senior manager at a life insurance company about training his staff. 'Lots of Independent Financial Advisors took this profession because of the lifestyle it offered,' he told me. 'Now, most of them are so taken up with the lifestyle that they have lost their motivation for work and lost sight of why they are here and the people they are here to serve.' Put another way: Do we get so focused on what we are taking out of a job that we lose focus of what we are putting in?

As Christians we are called to focus on what we give, not what we receive. In that way, we can reflect our calling in any job we do. Grasping this attitude to work may be one of the most significant changes in our ability to love work and live life. It's all too easy to become dissatisfied and disillusioned if we believe that our calling or our vocation is to be found somewhere else, with someone else, doing something else. This is like chasing the pot at the end of the rainbow – we will never find the gold and in the process, with the enemy clapping and cheering us on, God's people will miss the purpose and beauty in the rainbow. That for me is the starting point to loving work and living life – settling the issue that whatever the future holds I can and in fact must serve God here, now, doing whatever it is that I am doing.

But does everyone get a specific calling to their job?

Rob Parsons once told me a story about a young man called Tom. Tom came to Cardiff homeless, selling copies of *The Big Issue*, living in the back of a van. Someone from a local church contacted Care for the Family to see if they had any jobs Tom could do to earn a better living. Eventually Tom was given the job of data entry. However, it soon became apparent that Tom had hidden talents. Not only did he have a degree in anthropology but he'd also been involved in the ANC negotiations in South Africa. Keen to see Tom fulfil his potential, Rob asked him if he would like to be a researcher helping Care for the Family with various projects. To Rob's slight annoyance Tom said, 'Can I have a week to pray about it?'

A week later Rob approached Tom again. 'What did God say?'

'Well,' said Tom, 'I asked God if I should stay in data entry or take the job in research and God said, you choose, either's fine with me.'

The fact is, sometimes God does speak to individuals in quite dramatic ways about their jobs. But most of the time God simply leaves it to the desires of our hearts.

In the seminars we run for Care for the Family, we often ask our audience this question: 'If your job could be anything you want, what would it be?' Amusingly, people often say, 'I don't know.' Our response is always, 'Well if you did know what would it be?' The reason we ask this particular question is that it is one of a number of useful indicators about possible combinations of gifting, natural talent and simple desire. Can it be that simple? Yes it can. If God gives us the desire of our hearts, then if our motives are straightforward, an answer to a question like this can be a mirror into our soul – we get a glimpse of what our heart does really desire and it's usually a reflection of what God himself has already put in there.

Different callings

At this point there might just be a question running around inside your head about all those clear callings we read about in the Bible. Joseph, Elisha, Elijah, Jeremiah and Samuel, all had remarkable and quite specific callings. But these are the encounters we remember because they were dramatic. What about Daniel? He simply let his character and gifts open up doors for him. His ministry started not with a divine encounter but with refusal to eat foods! Zechariah, who as a young man wrote down what he saw and God took it and used it. He didn't have a call to write Scripture. He simply used the gift God had given.

People have often asked me the question, 'How do I discover my destiny in God?' Much is made of one passage in Philippians which says, 'I press on to take hold of that for which Christ Jesus took hold of me.' I have met thousands of people from different cultures and different generations who are longing to find *that* – the one thing that God has apparently called them to. But if we start by suggesting that every Christian should have a supernatural call, we run a real danger of bringing disillusionment to the many, whilst releasing and enthusing the few.

For years there had been a certain restlessness in me, constantly looking for the 'that' to which God had called me. I even had a dream that I thought might be God trying to connect me to that one thing he wanted me to do. The dream wasn't complicated, but it was clear. In it I saw one image, the Greek capital letter 'sigma' or 'Σ'. However, try as I might, I couldn't come up with a connection between the dream and this restless pursuit for, 'the one big thing'.

I recall standing in line at the theatre with some friends, Dave and Elaine, later that day and found myself sharing the dream. Dave said, 'Let's ring my son Andrew and ask him what sigma means.' Andrew's answer was straightforward. 'It means the 'sum of all the parts'. Armed with this insight I began to pray once more. And as I prayed I sensed God saying to me, 'You are looking for that one thing. But son, it's not one thing, your destiny is the sum of all the parts. It's the sum of all you have done so far, all you are doing now and all that I will yet lead you into.' I can't tell you what an utter relief it was to be free from this relentless dissatisfying pursuit for one big thing.

Spiritual DNA

If we are not one of those who have had a specific calling, what do we do? The Bible itself gives us another clue. Our natural DNA determines our skin colour, our gender and the colour of our eyes; all those things are 'written into us'. In the same way there is another type of DNA which has to do with purpose, function, and destiny. The Bible talks about the fact that there are days ordained and there are works ordained. This is one reason why, as Christians, we often get a strong inner restlessness – a godly dissatisfaction. In Psalm 139, God talks about 'knitting us' with stitches that contain the blueprint of this function, our ministry and our destiny. If you like, a spiritual DNA. We cannot be a human being without having DNA. We cannot be a child of God without having spiritual DNA written into our beings by a loving God.

Here, then, we face our first dilemma. Most of us know, or at least hope, that God has a special plan or purpose for our destiny and for our lives – but how do we discover and fulfil it? One thing is certain: this destiny will not just unfold – this will require our active participation and cooperation.

Someone once described eternal life as 'finding the will of God and doing it now'. God wants our lives resonating with purpose and divine activity. He wants us to see, believe and act upon the truth of our importance, our meaning, our value and our relevance. The big question is, how do I seek it, find it, discover it? Thankfully, while there is work for us to do, the answer isn't rocket science. It begins with the primary command of Jesus – seek first the kingdom of God. We all know this is Jesus' primary teaching to us and yet many, if not most of us, are vague in our ability to implement this call and genuinely apply it to ourselves. In most cases, it is not out of disobedience, but rather a lack of knowing exactly what it means.

Having talked with thousands of Christians over the last 20 years, it is clear to me that there are two things which Christians invariably find it hard to do:

1. Know the will of God.
2. Find the kingdom of God.

We want to follow Jesus and we want to be obedient, but we can't understand how to make the kingdom of God relevant in our own lives. We know we should look for it, but we don't know where! The question is – has Jesus given us the address?

Our friends, Phillip and Joanna, had a new house. We knew it existed, we knew they had purchased it, we had seen pictures of it and heard people talk about it – but we couldn't find it because we didn't have the address! We drove round their village for ages looking blindly for the place. That's how it is for many of us – we search for the kingdom, we have some Bible pictures of it, others have talked about it, but we seem to wander round and round wishing we could find it. It's like looking for buried treasure by digging up any and every bit of soil that we come across, only to discover after years of frustration that we had the map in our possession which gave us the precise location.

Jesus tells us where and how to find the kingdom. He says that people will not say 'here it is' or 'there it is', because the kingdom of God is – where? Within you (or among you)! We don't find it because we are looking 'out there' instead of starting 'in here'.

Finding our calling in our gifts

God in his grace has gifted us all. Not for our own benefit or personal blessing. These gifts are a deposit of the kingdom of God. These gifts are one of God's primary ways of bringing his kingdom into our world. As we seek and discover the unique blend of gifts that God has given us we will begin to discern our unique destiny. But most important of all, as we put our gifts to work, the kingdom of God will open up before us.

As we seek God for the gifts he has given, we find that our spiritual DNA is encapsulated in these gifts within us. As we seek and begin to use them, our destiny begins to emerge. The stressful habit of constantly looking for God's ultimate will becomes reversed. We find the seeds of God's will in the gifts he has placed within us.

The X factor

In Jesus' parable of the talents, we have another clear indication of how to discover and respond to the will of God in terms of work, vocation or call. You remember the story – the servant with five talents puts them to work and gains five more, the one with two does the same but the one with just one talent hides it and makes nothing of it and then is surprised when he gets taken to task as 'wicked, lazy, worthless' by his master. Using this parable, the theologian, Calvin, shaped the modern meaning of the words talent and talented. Like many theologians after him, Calvin believed that in every human being lies a range of talents or inherent skills that we are 'called' to put to work. These inherent skills, attributes and abilities are what some business trainers call 'Factor X'. The question is: How can we find this Factor X, this doing what we do best?

I want to give you encouragement and permission to experiment. One of the most common ways to find out what your Factor X is, is by discovering what it is not. Be free to 'get it wrong' and enjoy the process of discovery. If we could see the search for our Factor X as a journey on which it is inevitable and necessary that we discover what it isn't then we take pressure off ourselves. We need to plan a journey that takes that into account. In my family, two of our kids knew, and we knew, exactly what their Factor X was. With the other two we didn't and nor did they. Real life seems to be roughly in that proportion. It's as if some, around half in fact, are born with a single key and just about everyone can see where it fits early on in life.

Others of us are born with a bunch of keys and the journey for both is equally valid but totally different. If you are amongst those born with a set of keys let me encourage you to try. Let me encourage you – if you are in the 50 per cent that don't know – enjoy the journey and find out, with adventure, what it isn't as you also discover what it is. Who knows what fabulous possibilities lie in you as you search this out. Who knows what amazing horizons of possibility lie ahead!

So it is that we remind ourselves that in Scripture some had a supernatural calling, but many did not. I think the majority had natural abilities which they put to work together with the spiritual giftings they carried.

God does not give us talents without expecting us to use them.

God does not give us gifts without expecting us to exercise them.

The desires of our hearts, in most people, reflect a combination of both.

Practical applications

I have expressed my profound conviction that we find God's calling for our lives as we discover the gifts that he has placed within us and look for the talents and skills he has invested in us. God is good – his calling and his gifting go together. He does not tear us apart by calling us into areas where we are not gifted.

But two words of caution. First, let me go right back to the beginning. We find the call of God right where we are, in the job we are doing right now. If we refuse to accept that we are where we are through the loving providence of God, and work as well as we can in that place, then we may not be ready to be called out to new places where our gifts can be more fully expressed.

The second point leads on from this. Gifts can only be fully used for God's service when we have offered them to God and are prepared to use them in his strength. This cuts two ways. We might be like Moses, initially afraid of using his speaking ability, but gradually equipped to do so more and more as he dared to go out and face his fears with God. But we might also be tempted to use our God-given gift for our own purposes, not God's. Then God might need to teach us that without him we can do nothing, whatever our gifting.

You and I will never fully love work and live life until we know our strengths and our gifts and find those who allow us to use them. But hurry, time is short. As Rob Parsons quotes in his great book *The Heart of Success*, Quentin Crisp was right, 'It's no good running a pig farm badly for 30 years while saying, "Really I was meant to be a ballet dancer." By that time pigs will be your style.'

4.

God's Gift to Work

Our God-given gifts are not just about finding the work God has called us to do, but about shaping and flavouring that job so that we play a unique role as Christians in the workplace, bringing God and his kingdom to others. Below are some real stories about ordinary people who have changed the workplace by being open to using the gifts God has given them.

Teaching at work

I know countless scores of men and women who have a teaching gift. The state school system is a place where Christians with gifting and vision can really make a difference, and many do. One of my friends, David Robotham, has been a teacher in the state sector – in fact he was a very successful headmaster. He has also run two schools in Africa. Let me quote from his written school philosophy from the International School of South Africa:

> The school has a Christian foundation . . . our Christianity governs our relationships. Self-sacrificing love is its foundation, and mutual respect for cultures, religions and people of different backgrounds is its outcome.

As God's church, we need to have a real and ongoing passion to see a whole new generation of teachers who can bring God's voice into our schools and education system. There is a need to support the faithful men and women who have faithfully taught for many years, through major changes in education. But there is also a need to pray for a whole new generation of visionary men and women who can be part of God's new wave into education. We need to encourage them to be the gift they were created to be in this tough and demanding job.

Being pastoral at work

Margaret Veitch expresses her pastoral gifts in the hospice at Basingstoke, which provides an incredible level of care for the terminally ill. Pain relief, palliative care for other forms of distress and suffering, personal love and unstinting devotion are all part of Margaret's daily job.

Another remarkable woman is Joanna Thompson. She started by simply asking God what he wanted this 'little housewife', as she calls herself, to do. Today, she has an overseeing role with over one hundred Pregnancy Crisis Centres in the UK. Her first now sees over one thousand women each year. Joanna has been involved a number of times on prime-time TV and she speaks in Europe and South Africa, and has found herself advising MPs in Sweden. As Joanna put her gifting to work, God enlarged the horizons of her application.

The servant leader

There is one example that springs irrepressibly to my mind, combining a leadership gifting with a serving gift. The example is Jonathan Booth at Care for the Family. He has an outstanding gift of leadership but also has an amazing capacity for service. Some years back, Jonathan sensed that God had called him to serve Rob Parsons, specifically enabling Rob's ministry to be expressed to the full. That serving leadership has enabled Rob to speak to hundreds of thousands of people about family and life issues and enabled Care for the Family to grow from two people working out of a bedroom, to the organisation it is today.

I was once with Jonathan as he sat at the back of St Aldate's Church, Oxford. He had driven up from Cardiff to be with Rob as he addressed the crowded room full of parents. I expected

Jonathan to be hosting the evening as he often does so well with Care for the Family, but when I asked he grinned and said, 'No I'm just here to be with Rob.' As I left that evening, I reflected to myself. If Jonathan did not do what he did, Rob would not be doing what he does with the same breadth, power and frequency.

Administration

I watch with interest another friend at Care for the Family – Ian Purcell. Ian works as the Special Assistant to the Director of Care for the Family. I've had the pleasure of working with Ian recently. During that time he has been tireless in his consistent attention to detail. Ian has never once in that time flapped, never once let a careless word out of his lips, never once implied that what I was asking was an overload or irritation even though I have been aware of colossal stress. He has never once spoken ill of his boss and is always a positive contributor to ideas and concepts. He believes God has called him to be a number two – someone who supports the front runner and is content to serve with excellence in that capacity. Ian is an accountant by training but has chosen to live out his administrative gift in this setting.

Evangelism

Malcolm Murray is a leader. He has been a good MD of several companies. Right now he is Sales Director of a very successful company. The thing is, along with his leadership, is an irrepressible gift that evangelises in all kinds of ways.

Malcolm is never afraid to talk about his faith or the church he attends to whoever he meets, whether they be colleagues or clients. When someone asks him about his weekend he always takes the opportunity to talk about church and his faith in God.

Ever since I have known Malcolm, I have seen him naturally, inoffensively talking over meals, sharing at Christmas parties and sales meetings. Never once has anyone complained or said that he was preaching at them. In fact quite the opposite – many would talk for hours. It's strange for me. I just don't have the same ability nor do I get the same results. Both Malcolm and I share sales and marketing skills, but this is a gift he has which I do not possess and he puts that gift consistently, naturally and seamlessly to work.

Being prophetic

1 Chronicles talks about the prophet bringing practical solutions for success. So, imagine this boardroom scene in a city corporation. Round the table, John the MD is visibly perspiring, he is nervous that he can't see the solution to the pressing problem. The two longest serving members, Tina and George, tap their pencils in an agitated state of reflection – the impasse seems set to take them down, the answer seems so elusive and the silence in the boardroom is almost heart stopping. Then Peter speaks. Very quietly and with confidence he suggests two strategic changes that no one else had even considered. A tangible sense of relief fills the room and the chairman turns to Peter, 'Where did you get those ideas from?' Peter smiles to himself as he recalls with gratitude and amusement the house group last night where they prayed for him and encouraged him to trust and call on the prophetic gift within him.

Prophets also call out for integrity and righteousness. One of my favourite clients was Nick Robinson, the former chairman of the Marketing Guild. Whenever he introduced me, he introduced me as the 'company conscience'. I treasure that title more than any other I have been given or have taken! In one issue of the Guild's newsletter, there was an article which I felt was inappropriate. Nick disagreed with my judgement but nonetheless printed an apology and gave my point of view. I appreciated that approach.

Prophetic people are responsible for equipping others for works of service, which invariably involves helping them to discover who they are and what gifting they have. The various workplace seminars run by Care for the Family are part of that process of discovery.

Healing

I have a friend, Steve Woods, who is one of the best intensive care nurses I know. He is also absolutely brilliant at terminal care. In fact, when my close friend Dave Marchment was in his final weeks, it was Steve who supervised the home-based care and made sure he was pain free and that the family were postured for the process and the outcomes. His gift is awesome. The problem is, with the cost of housing in Hampshire, he cannot provide adequately for his family on a nurse's salary. So, what Steve has done is to take a job in a medical company and then do additional work as a bank nurse so that he can continue to use his God-given gift.

Another friend is Christine Ball. She has been physio to the UK's bob sleigh team and she runs her own physio practice. I suffer from a weak back and whenever it has gone over the years she has been able to sort it – speedily and with amazingly long-term results. I have recommended scores of people to her and there is an intangible quality to her work that I am convinced is God working through her.

I have only been able to highlight a few examples here of how God uses our gifts to shape and impact our workplace through us. There are countless ways in which our gifts, ministries and natural talents can be expressed with joy and faith into the world of work. These examples are a tiny proportion of what can be done by stewarding our gifts and talents. As we do that on the shop floor, in school, on the wards, in fire engines, behind desks, in hotel conference rooms, let's remember that we are in partnership with an infinitely creative God and let's look to him to bless our life, our gifts and our natural abilities.

Love 'Church' Work

5.

Love Work? Love the Church!

It's obvious to us all that the western church, with some notable exceptions, is in trouble. It has reached an impasse. It is simply not succeeding in its work of bringing the kingdom of God to earth. My desire is to face this impasse head-on. The easy option would be simply to tear down the buildings, forsake the gatherings and send the pastors and priests packing. Truth is, we would be far worse off if we did that. Somehow, as workers and church leaders alike, we need to search for new ways of being church, in which we can use our God-given resources strategically and effectively. Before we do that, however, we need to work through the impasse. If this does not happen we will succeed only in rearranging the furniture once again.

The church is no accident for people at work

Ephesus was the most important town in Asia Minor, now Turkey. It had a harbour that opened into the Caystem River, which in turn emptied into the Aegean Sea. It had few equals anywhere in the world. Certainly no city in Asia was more famous or more populous – it ranked with Rome, Corinth, Antioch and Alexandria as one of the main urban centres of the empire. It is into this modern, successful, cultural, political and economic environment that Paul writes with power about God's plan for the church, God's view of the church, and the church's role. In Matthew's Gospel, Jesus gives a name to his plan for our world – and that name is 'church'.

What does the name 'church' mean? Most of you probably know this well. In the Greek, the word is *Ekklesia* (*Ek* means 'out of'; *Klesis* means 'a calling'). It was used in ordinary Greek language to describe a group of citizens who were gathered to discuss the affairs of state. But when the word is used in Matthew, and then throughout the New Testament, it has a much more significant and precise meaning. A meaning that gives every Christian an identity, an environment and a definition. It is never used to describe a building. It is not meant to describe a meeting – we don't go to church, we are the church. It is not meant to describe a denomination, group or stream. When we become a Christian, we are added to the church and we are 'called out' – called out of darkness, called out of being self-sufficient and called into God's church – a new world, a new environment with wonderful promises, protection, provision and responsibilities. Whether we like it or not, whether we know it or not, we're in God's church and nothing is going to change that.

The church is strategic

As God's church we should not be on the defensive all the time but on the offensive. The church's role is not to sit and wait and hope to defend. The church's role is to act positively to change lives, to change communities, to change whole societies – even to change the workplace!

The church is described as 'the pillar and foundation of truth'. Spoken truth is supported, and given substance, by the church. God does not have an alternative, this is the plan that is to work and will work. Look at Eph. 1:22,23: 'And he put all things under his feet, and gave him to be head over all things to the church, which is his body, the fullness of him who fills all in all.'

We are the expression on earth of his fullness. He has no other body to express it through except us – the church. We are his arms, his legs; we are his physical presence on the earth. We are the light of the world, we are the salt of the earth – there is no other. In other words, the name 'church' is given to the life and works of God's people not meetings, not leadership teams or their programmes. The church is the people that God has called out and gathered, not to a meeting but to himself and to each other, and to a life of purpose and good works.

The church and me

There is no concept in the New Testament of a successful, 'churchless' walk with God. The two appear contradictory. I need the church and the church needs me. You need the church and the church needs you!

If I try to pursue what I term my 'calling' or role in the kingdom of God – business, medicine, marriage, family, education – without God's people the church challenging, affirming, supporting, encouraging or without total involvement, I will almost definitely begin to struggle along the route, becoming barren, dry and sceptical – eventually losing heart and becoming apathetic.

In Ephesians, Paul cries out, 'that you may know that to which he has called you – the riches of his glorious inheritance in the Saints'. Paul makes it clear that we are called to the church.

I am not called exclusively to education, to the shop floor, to business, to politics or to social action. I am called to the church, and as the church I shall be equipped and sent out to do God's work in these fields: supported, strengthened, encouraged, confronted and prayed over.

Paul goes on to make it clear that when we attempt to follow God's will, there will be difficulties and strife. Our struggle is not always against flesh and blood but against the rulers, against the authorities, against the power of this dark world and against the spiritual forces of evil in the heavenly realms. You can't make it for ever on your own. In the prayer that was to be a model for every day, Jesus taught 'lead us not into temptation but deliver us from evil'. We are not called to handle these things on our own.

George Eldon Ladd described the kingdom and the church as follows:

> The kingdom creates the church, works through the church and is proclaimed in the world by the church. There can be no kingdom without a church (those who have acknowledged God's rule) and there can be no church without God's kingdom; but they remain

two distinguishable concepts – the rule of God and the fellowship of men.

I would add that there can be no concept of my calling to work without that fellowship of people.

The church and its resources

In Ephesians, Paul talks quite clearly about us 'being created in Christ Jesus to do good works which God prepared in advance for us to do'. Those good works can be a whole variety of things, but will certainly include our roles at home, in business, in the caring professions, in education, in the family, in social action and politics.

In the church, God has appointed first of all apostles, prophets, teachers, miracle-workers, healers, and administrators and so on. These gifts are the method by which Jesus builds the church. These gifts are there to prepare God's people for works of service. But what I want to suggest is that works of service shouldn't be limited to church gatherings. Our times together as a church may well provide a place where we can serve – but most of our time is spent away from church, in our places of work, with family and friends, and these are places also where we need to learn to serve others with the gifts God has given us.

In the past two decades, much of our focus, our measure of value and most of our resources have centred on church gatherings and church activity. But the Bible is not a book centred on the church in its gathered form. The Bible is a book about men and women at work, written in part by men and women, for ordinary working people like you and I. And in those places of work we need God's provision to help us be the church to others.

A sitting lunch for wolves

Without the church I am a sitting lunch for the 'savage wolves'. Paul says to the elders of the Ephesian church, 'I know after I leave, savage wolves will come in among you and will not spare the flock'. If we have an incorrect concept of, or an incorrect attitude towards, the church, we are easy pickings for the savage wolves. Note the plural – wolves. As Jesus said, these ferocious wolves can come in sheep's clothing, so that you never know their identity until it's too late.

I love to visit the Savannah and Veldt areas of Africa whenever I travel there. I love to watch the majesty of the predators. I love to watch hunting dogs take down the mighty wildebeest. I love to watch the natural world documentaries on the TV. I was reminded of this chapter, when watching a pack of small wolves take down a massive and impressive buffalo. How do small, insignificant creatures take down such an animal? It is so simple. They watch for one on the edge of the herd. He is so self-assured, so confident that his strength is adequate! All they do is constantly nip at his heels. At first he hardly notices. Then he gets irritated and begins to kick back almost half-heartedly. Then they do it so constantly that they do not let him eat or drink. After several days he begins to tire, and after a few more days he stumbles and the wolves have him. They sink their teeth into the neck, the blood spurts and it's all over.

I wonder if you are on the edge of the herd? I wonder if the wolves are already nipping at your legs? I wonder if they have already stopped you eating and drinking? How will you know? Here are ten possible warning symptoms:

1. A gradual and increasing preoccupation with things outside the church, to the increasing exclusion of the church – in particular work or home.
2. Sterile, barren, fruitless, dry or dusty walk with God. Bible and prayer probably partly neglected, but apparently valueless! Heavens feel like brass.
3. Growing dislike of time with other Christians or growing reluctance to spend time with them.
4. Increasing retreat into your own world, which brings detachment, loneliness, isolation or independence. This is rarely wilful but by default. You probably don't actually like this experience, but find it difficult to force your way back into fellowship.
5. Increasing success in the area of preoccupation.

6. Increasing wealth – less need of God and his church; thanksgiving gets less and consumption gets more; giving is out of guilt or increased stinginess.

7. Increased levels of temptation in areas like sex, materialism and new philosophies such as New Age.

8. No operation of the gifts of the Spirit.

9. Increased confidence and reliance on your own strength and your own abilities.

10. Where once you led God's people, you now sit in passive, mediocre neutrality.

6.

Supporting the Church with Work-Based Skills

I can't count the number of times a business person has told me things that they can see wrong in their church. They usually tell me with a sigh – a weary, 'why can't they see it?' kind of sigh. The implication is that their successful work environment, their earned respect at work, is somehow the basis for an automatic right to speak into the church, see its faults and provide the remedies. The working person who has no real root in the church, the working person who has not resolved that issue, is like a disconnected eye. You can see all you want, but you will never successfully communicate that back to the body because the effective connection is simply not there. The danger with this, is that there will come an increasing estrangement with the risk that you will say things you regret and become over-critical and cynical, which may affect others.

Time, please

It has been said that these days Christians will part with everything except their time. That has proved to be frighteningly true. How about a challenge to bring our time under the lordship of Christ?

At Basingstoke Community Church, once a year the leaders take 2 or 3 days out for prayer and strategy review. As part of that review, each leader is required to share what his or her workload is and what he or she is doing with their time. It is a very healthy exercise where corporate prayer and wisdom nearly always challenges us as to the use of our time resulting in a re-commitment to adjust our time management accordingly.

One of the ways to get support if you are a busy individual, with a number of consuming responsibilities, is to sit down with your pastors or fellow leaders and say, 'Look, this is what I do. Here are my responsibilities. Please help me weigh them up – am I following God or am I being duped?' One of the most meaningful things you can subsequently do is to say, 'Look, this is the likely time I will have available. What are your priorities for the time that I can give?' In other words, let your fellow elders or your pastor have input into deciding what you give your time to.

How to support with care

There have been a number of times over the years where I have endeavoured to help in a church situation, only to sense some resistance. Why? Well in nearly every case it has been my attitude, the way I have come across, the spirit in which I am operating. Typically, in my case, people perceive me as forceful, unyielding, impatient, arrogant, perhaps even condescending. Why would I be like that? Well, because I am expecting the same response as I would get in the office that I run, or from the clients who pay for my advice. They are two totally different spheres of government and I cannot approach one, necessarily, in the same way as the other.

Business can be so wonderfully pragmatic, so ordered, so structured. It is easy for me as a businessman to move in my own strength, my own authority. How is that reflected?

- Impatience with church members and their lack of commitment.
- Impatience with church leaders and their inability to make decisions in a reasonable length of time.
- An arrogant devaluing of what church leaders do – thinking that it is trivial.
- Rushing to get away from meetings because I have something more practical, more real, more valuable to do.

Very often the leaders in our churches have left well-paid, well-structured, reassuring working lives, to take up the lowly-paid, insecure and fickle world of serving the church. They don't have the money we do, they don't have the parameters of success that we so often have. They don't have a lot of things that we do. If we could love them, if we could serve them with a serving heart, if we could commit our time to them in ways which are helpful to them, we could support them with much greater care.

How Jesus used work-experience to build the church

In Jewish culture, it was said that a man was teaching his son to steal if he did not teach his son a trade by the age of 12. We know from that, and from the reference in Mark's Gospel, that Jesus would have been apprenticed as a carpenter and was known for his activity in that realm. Most Bible teachers agree with the suggestion that Joseph probably died during Jesus' teenage years. That, by inference, would mean that Jesus, as the oldest son, would have taken a leading role in the family business from an early age. Therefore, much of what Jesus learned about life would have come from his work-experience. Where else do you think he learned to understand people, read them and know them? Where else did he get his remarkable ability to understand ordinary men and women? Where else do you think he discovered the value of being able to handle success and failure? – something he was keen to teach his disciples.

Jesus carried what he learned from his work-experience as a carpenter into his working ministry as he moved from building boats and furniture to building his church. Understanding ordinary working life made him the great teacher of ordinary working people that he was. There was no sacred/secular divide as far as Jesus was concerned – and so there shouldn't be one for us.

What were the ingredients that made work and church seamless for Jesus?

- He always sought to do the Father's will.
- He utilised the gifts God the Father had given him in every environment.
- He prayed constantly.

These were the ingredients that enabled him to learn or develop all these work-based skills and attributes. These were the ingredients with which Jesus built his church.

Building with Jesus

There are all kinds of ways in which our work-based skills can bring success and resource the church: Alpha group leading, coaching, mentoring or discipling, leadership, hospitality, intercessory prayer, evangelism, teaching, pastoring, counselling, accounting, fund-raising, legal work, charitable work, copy writing, promotion, accounts, project management, administration, stewarding, cooking, DIY, work with children and teenagers, pregnancy counselling, giving regularly and sacrificially, and so on.

Clearly, this list is not exhaustive, and includes a mix of practical talents along with spiritual gifts.

Corporate responsibility

Both working men and women and the church leadership are jointly responsible before God to steward their gifts, talents and resources. Church leaders need to preach and teach about stewardship of time and resource, about God-given gifts and natural talent, and call church members to use their giftedness to the full.

Every man or woman who has ever heard the parable of the talents knows the principle of putting your two to work to gain two more, and putting your five to work to gain five more. But bury the one that you have, in other words, don't actively seek to put it to work in your working world or your church gatherings, then nothing good can come of it. God wants us to take the principle of active participation – sacrificial participation – very seriously.

7.

Reflecting Reality in Our Churches

If we have been duped into falling for the sacred/secular myth for decades, if our hearts and minds have been taught that the pastor and the missionary do the holy work, if we have been inseminated with the idea that certain types of work intrinsically carry more value than others, then it's little wonder that our churches don't exactly resonate with relevance to the average outsider. 'New' churches and traditional churches, it seems to me, vary little on this score.

This has combined with a view of church which has tended to limit the belief of responsibility. Most of our congregations believe that we are the church when we are together in the building, we are the church when we are operating together in the neighbourhood, we are the church when we are gathered together or involved in foreign mission. But do not believe that we are the church when we are scattered in the world. Then we are on our own. Individuals are salt, but they are not the church!

Supporting working men and women

As church leaders, if we won't or don't change, then Christianity will become increasingly marginalised in the workplace, and our church gatherings and structures will become increasingly irrelevant to everyday people in normal occupations.

If the world of work is to be transformed, then something more than a developed doctrine of employment and vocation is needed. If not us, who? If not now, when?

Working men and women have a knowledge that there is more, a hunger to see more and in many cases a commitment to press through for more. How can we partner them? My question is this: Can we change our practical support so that we can help to facilitate the integration of faith and work, so that our people feel their value and believe in their calling, so they can live the gospel of the kingdom, apply the gospel of the kingdom and share the gospel of the kingdom?

Taking a reality check

Before any specific changes are contemplated, the elders, minister and leadership team need to know clearly in their own minds what they believe and to discuss the implications. A change of thinking, a real change of thinking, will require a change in response, priorities and action.

Church notices are a mirror. They are a mirror into the reflected beliefs of those in charge. As I write this chapter, on my desk I have notices from various different churches. I have counted 59 pages of notices in total, with just 39 lines that could be linked with the world of work. Those 39 lines take up less than one page. Compare that with 21 pages of notices for meetings and 10 pages of items for sale!

How about starting here, ensuring that our notices include the world of work? How about a testimony from shop floor, office or hospital ward? An encouragement each week on some work-related principle? While we are at it, how about a section each week devoted to the young people at school, college and university? And how about a sentence or two for unpaid workers like housewives or single parents?

Church meetings and gatherings need to be reviewed. We all need to think through this question: Are our meetings really there to serve working men and women, or are they simply serving the meeting?

Leaders and their place in the world of work

I shall never forget the tears and the air of bleak disappointment mixed with the presence of God. One of my friends, who had had a thriving, successful business, had been forced into liquidation. Though there was nothing that could be done to save the business, my friend wanted to ensure that there were people around to support the staff emotionally and with prayer. So several leaders from my friend's church gathered at the office to be available to talk with, listen to, support and pray for his staff at this most difficult time. Though many of the staff weren't Christians, they truly appreciated this support.

Sadly, in my experience, such a supportive encounter between work and church is a rare experience. I know one or two church groups have had the occasional foray into the world of businessmen. I'm all for that, but let's think of creative ways in which we could interact with all types of working men and women. In what creative ways could a pastor, minister or church leader adopt the same spirit or stance?

For years, my mentor and spiritual dad, Ron Trudinger, used to travel with me every week or so when I was a travelling salesman. He used to sit in the car while I made the visit, pray for a successful sale and then we would enjoy lunch or dinner together. Those times were memorable: we would laugh, we would pray, he would sharpen some area of my life, my work, my family or my preaching, and they were such enjoyable, productive days.

As working people we need to think of creative ways in which we could invite other church member to meet our colleagues, visit our workplace, have lunch or whatever?

David Marchment, formerly Senior Pastor at Basingstoke Community Church, said:

> Having been a teacher for 6 years, I do remember well the pressures of that particular workplace. I often wonder, having served the Lord for 20 years in the employ of the church, whether regular time immersed in the 'marketplace' might be very good for all church staff, to help keep them informed and in touch with their congregations. The local Baptist church pastor had a sabbatical and spent quite a bit of that time talking to 'all and sundry' in a local financial institution. He was shocked by the pressures many people are facing and had the opportunity to pray, and weep, with many of them! On occasion, I have 'shadowed' members of the church for a day, and often arrange to 'visit people' at their place

of work during the lunch-break. I have never failed to be thanked and appreciated when I have done this. Hazel, my wife, has done a similar thing with some of the ladies, and has been met with a deluge of thanks and requests for repeat visits!

How to lead with confidence

In my experience church leaders want to change and want to help but they are unsure of just how to do it. One of the keys in my experience is that many lack confidence. They can often feel quite intimidated. It may be years since they were in that kind of working world, if ever. I have often approached church leaders to come and minister in the working environment only to have them say, 'I don't know if what I've got is relevant', or 'I don't know if I have anything to offer'.

I want to speak loud and clear to every church leader: You will feel awkward, and you will probably feel inadequate to help a banker, medic, staff nurse, headmaster or stay-at-home mum. But in that moment of weakness, genuine weakness, lies an open doorway. If you will pluck up the courage to walk through that doorway with your weakness, feeling intimidated – not really sure if you have anything to offer – then it may just be that God's strength can begin to operate through you.

In practical terms, don't feel under pressure to have lots of answers, or even any answers. It's enough that you are involved and what has great value is the affirmation that you bring. This process is like the day you start a new job. There is apprehension and actually the best thing to do is to let others lead you and have questions ready to learn. Every relationship and working environment will be different, with different opportunities and stress points. If I could encourage you, let the process develop and don't expect too much too soon. But do let it be known that you are willing to stay involved for as long as it is helpful. This is a journey of discovery, learning what it might mean to genuinely equip saints for their works of service in their world in a way that is meaningful to them.

When one friend heard that I was going to address this issue in the book he phoned me to make this encouraging comment:

A trusted ear is an incredibly valuable and rare thing. The ability to share openly, knowing it's going no further, carries great value for me and for people like me who carry responsibilities. The time together can be a check and balance – an informal opportunity for accountability. It also facilitates time for fellowship and friendship. Leaders should be encouraged not to underestimate the value of moments like these for workplace people, especially for leaders in the workplace. These times help you as a leader to understand the environment in which your people operate; it gives a genuine feel for the context. And there is nothing like a personal touch to engage more effectively in ongoing care and prayer, affirmation and encouragement.

Changing the way we preach

Our church gatherings are seldom, it seems, geared to the realities of the working men and women who attend them. So what can we do about changing our gatherings? The answers may be simple. We can start with a genuine attitude of affirmation and encouragement. We can routinely make room for contributions from our working men and women and treat them as meaningful and as important as any other form of contribution.

In his great resource *Supporting Christians in the Workplace*, my friend Mark Greene suggests taking workplace people away for an evening or a Saturday several times a year, and either asking them what issues they would like taught in the coming 6 months, or telling them what you as a leadership team are hoping to teach – then asking them for input with real life challenges or stories.

Perhaps the most important thing we can do, however, would be to preach like Jesus preached. For whenever Jesus preached, he secured and held the attention of his listeners. He would establish a point of contact and then appeal to something familiar, slap-bang up to date and relevant to the daily news or their own realm of work or experience. His messages were infused with regular, emotional life and experience. Jesus was regularly asking questions.

If we want ordinary working men and women to respond positively to our teaching and preaching, we might be well advised to ensure that we are answering questions they are asking, or at least a question in which they have the remotest interest! If the common people heard Jesus gladly it was because he was addressing things that were of common interest. Consider just a partial list of the topics his preaching covered – debt, money, work, family, fair pay, employment ethics, stewardship, taxes and anxiety. Jesus faced life and preached life in a gutsy, 'in your face' way. He drew vivid pictures from ordinary, everyday life.

Changing the way we pray

Have you ever heard a minister pray over the offering, saying, 'We often think of money as sordid, but you, Lord, have the ability to take what is sordid and turn it into something beautiful'? I remember similar prayers in my own experience of church in my youth. What does that say? What message does that send out?

Think of Laurie Deadman in my church, who has spent the week decorating people's homes. Think of Laurie Aldrich, who has spent a week, with overtime, working a lathe for Schlumberger. Think of Elaine Crick, a sister at the eye clinic in Basingstoke. What would that prayer do for them, as they devotedly bring their offerings, having slogged their guts out in hard, often manual work?

Every time we take tithes and offerings, I try to make a habit of thanking God for the money, thanking God for employment and asking God for work for our unemployed.

When you have a prayer time or an intercession evening, do you bring work-related issues into the prayer times? How about focusing on one group at a time, for example praying one evening for state school teachers, along with all the other issues?

How about bringing some variety into prayer times, like praying in large groups, led from the front, then breaking down into small groups and rotating those groups? Try to ensure that, each time, you pray for some work-related issues in those small groups.

In the cell group or house group, why not get each man or woman – one per week – to share about their work, specific challenges or opportunities and important relationships? Pray for those areas regularly.

David Marchment, wrote this:

> In 20 years, I have had to handle, and seek to help, many who have struggled, in one way or another, with their working environment. The issues have ranged from excessive pressures and deadlines, to verbal, physical and sexual abuse. Yet, even with the knowledge of all of this, it's easy for church staff to be so focused on the running of the church that church members who are facing daily pressures in the workplace can so easily feel misunderstood, ignored, or even irrelevant or insignificant . . . I now really appreciate the opportunity of simply listening to people talk about their work situations, and want to take the time to pray for people, and bless them in the name of Jesus for all they are doing.

Changing our language

What we name things – particularly as leaders – has a profound and disproportionate impact. If we as leaders call each other 'full-time' – for whatever reason – it can only demean others who are not fully-employed by the church.

My fear – particularly for leaders – is that in reality, by our words and by our priorities, we want our working men and women to see like we see, to feel like we feel, and to speak like we speak. Commitment then is not from us to them and on their behalf but in reality from them to us.

We say the church is not a building, we say the church does not consist of meetings. But look for a moment at the language of commitment we often employ. We ask for money for the upkeep of the building, commitment to meetings, commitment to home groups and commitment to church events. The language tells us what we really believe. How about a commitment course where the leadership team affirms the people's work and in which each of the leadership team commits themselves to equip each member for the works of service to which they are called. Where each member commits themselves not to church meetings, but to living out the kingdom of God in their place of work.

Why are there are so many discouraged weary, disillusioned – even defeated – teachers, medics and care workers? I'll tell you why. It's because while they are affirmed to some degree or other, they have not been fully affirmed to believe this is the highest calling possible for them. Their front line has not been held to be as important as the congregational activity around which they are still expected to gravitate.

I have really struggled with this one. With our own leaders, I have tried for years to get them to stop using the phrase 'full time'. They do try, but it regularly slips back into the language of the moment. It is easier than working hard to find a meaningful alternative. One of my friends, Dave Downer, asked, 'What do you call them, then?', acknowledging the practical need to have a working definition.

There are a number of choices, but how about 'church staff' or 'church-funded leaders'? We even tried 'LOGs' – those that Live Off the Gospel! One of the best solutions I have heard for this issue comes from Andrew Booth and his church in Fort Wayne – their leaders are called 'Ministry Coaches'. I think that's great because it is descriptive and it also gives a firm lead about who is serving whom.

Changing the teams that lead

I have been to more leaders' meetings than I've had hot dinners! Well, not exactly, but they do seem to crop up with incredible frequency. In the real world, the world where time is costed and weighed up in its use, meetings are quite interesting. Take a meeting with one of my clients. We had a meeting of seven highly-paid men and women. We started at 9:30 and by 11 the minutes were finished. We had twenty-five action points – most of which will be actioned by the next time we meet, in another month's time. I then spent 15 minutes with the MD talking about issues with six of his staff. Contrast that with the average church elders' meeting – 4 to 6 hours a week, with a budget a fraction of my client's. And if my experience from church audits is anything to go by, the same issues will be raised week after week, month after month and even year after year!

There are a handful of other working men in our elderships and I believe we are richer for it. When all you have on a leadership team or an eldership is church-paid staff, it can be incredibly unreal and not earthed. The inclusion of working men and women earths the team into reality. Churches that have moved away from working men and women in their core teams will, in my view, suffer in their relevance, their breadth and their effectiveness because they will lack elements of wisdom, prudence, faith and success.

Leaders and clergy, if you haven't already, make room for working men and women in your core team and get ready for some practical down-to-earth wisdom? After all, Solomon was amongst the wisest men ever to walk the face of this earth and his team was a mixture of paid staff and working men. But guess where the balance lay? If that was the wisest choice possible from the wisest man it should at least give us food for thought.

8.

A Radical Repackaging

Whilst visiting numerous church groups, I have the privilege of meeting quite often with different church leadership groups, elders and so on. It is quite common to see 'stuck' churches. By that, I mean godly men and women on church staff but with a fairly pedestrian level of church growth and life, and a certain local, parochial, even introspective, preoccupation. It has been extremely rare, in my twenty or so years of visiting churches, to see elders or ministries leaving church staff and going out to work in the real world. I find that quite strange – I really do. There is almost a panic alert when the possibility is mooted. At the same time, there are thousands of young men and women looking for room to express their fledgling leadership and ministries but, with great healthcare and an 80 per cent policy of dead man's shoes, little hope for them to be involved in any meaningful way. The sacred cow, I suspect, is, once on church staff, always on church staff.

Paul never had a calling to 'full-time ministry'. Paul never had a call to church staff. His call was as an apostle to the Gentiles. If that meant manufacturing with other workers for a season, fine. If it meant setting up a team to do that while he lectured at the local school, fine. But there was never an assumption that he was full-time church staff.

But that raises a question in my mind: Does God call any of us to a salaried position on church staff? Did he actually say, or even remotely infer, that this church staff position would eventually be with a pension and would be until retiring age? Or is it possible that he called you to a ministry that might just be more powerful if you had a job or a business which you ran? I know that this is a tough question, but I'm convinced it's one many of us should be asking ourselves. Perhaps it is time for all of us to revisit our calling and ask God, without fear, what it means in the light of understanding about full-time and church staff. Imagine the excitement if he said to you, 'Go and start a business, go and work in that school or go and nurse on that ward'? Wouldn't it be exciting to have to exercise our faith in a different new context? Wouldn't it be fantastic to have all that contact with non-Christians? Imagine how many others in your church or congregation would be called up, seriously involved, because you weren't available to do it all.

Let me share the story of a new friend of mine, Andrew Sercombe, he lives in the south of England, and this is what he writes:

> I will never forget the trauma of leaving the 'full-time Christian ministry'. I fulfilled all the negatives described on every psychometric test I've ever done. Pain, rejection, betrayal, disappointment and a whole lot more indescribable reactions swept over me, threatening to drown my shredded self-confidence for ever. The eighty-member village church, which we had started from scratch 15 years previously, became a source of deepest sadness for me. My decision to resign prevented further damage to me, to the family and to the innocent majority in the congregation who had little or no idea of what was going on.
>
> Looking back on that time towards the end of 1995, I can now see more clearly what was happening. The focus of my own vision had changed. I had become frustrated and disillusioned with the 'status quo', and I found myself in conflict with a handful of sincere, well-meaning people in our community church who wanted to keep things as they had been. I simply couldn't do that.
>
> So I was out, discovering a new world that seemed every bit as intimidating, challenging and seducing as that of the earliest explorers of America. A verse from the Bible became very important to me at that time. God was telling the Old Testament prophet Isaiah that he would make him 'a light to the nations'. I knew I could trust him to make me a 'light' to people in this different context. I felt quite strongly that I wanted to use the knowledge and experience I had gained in my past two careers – teaching design

and technology for 10 years and pastoring a church – to serve the business world. I wrote out a personal mission statement. It was a defining moment.

Naïve? You bet! It slowly dawned on me just how naïve I really was. I felt as if I had innocently bitten off far more than I could chew. This was an entirely different way of life! I had to learn and change to an entirely new language full of abbreviations, initials and business jargon I didn't understand. And I had to learn a substantially different culture. Having to market myself and charge for my time were major mountains to climb and utterly foreign to my past.

A lot of the time I was close to zero; pain and change were everywhere I looked. I had landed alone on a foreign shore. Yet I had to have answers and find where I fitted in. Inside I knew I actually did have those core answers, and would eventually gain the strength, skill and insight to make them real to others.

Slowly I managed to get some work. Redundancy workshops, communication skills workshops, supply teaching, one or two bits of simple 'consultancy', some personal coaching work; it slowly drifted in. I did various practical jobs to keep bread on the table, mending this and fixing that for people.

However, what I needed most was self-belief – to know and be confident in who I was, who God had made me to be, and confident with what I had learned over the previous 25 years of working with people, not just the last 2 or 3 years. Below the surface, I was maximising the first-hand experiences I would need for the future, not just learning about running a business, handling major change, the new order in the global corporate world, or 'lifetime learning', but experiencing what they really feel like, why they are important and how best to embrace them.

There are a lot of great people out there! Some helped because they loved us a lot and were simply genuine friends. I am sure some people helped me out of pity. Whatever! I needed every last bit of support I could get and I knew it. I was particularly grateful for those high up in the business world who believed in my vision, and mentored and educated me. It worked! People are starting to phone me instead of me phoning them. I no longer have the crippling desperation in my voice. We have managed to keep the house and stay free of major debt. But most important of all as far as I am concerned: the call on my life from many years ago to serve God 'full-time' remains utterly valid – and radically repackaged.

It might be God

I have watched with some interest some developing trends in the new churches that I work with. In many places, the leaders are still labelled 'the pastor' and my observation is that, particularly in our current low commitment culture, this pastor is increasingly becoming a 'clergyman'. He or she is increasingly doing the bulk of the work and increasingly feeling the weight of all that – pastoral work, studying, preaching, taking responsibility for leaders' meetings and Sunday gatherings. Concurrent with this is financial pressure. Increased UK house prices mean that many of these good men and women simply cannot make ends meet on the salary that the local church can pay them. Already a few of my friends in these roles are taking paid consultancy perhaps one or two days per week and for me the outcome is good to observe. In my observation, they are richer for the experience and more grounded. They are granted a different and higher level of respect because of such experience. A hidden value is that increasingly it will mean that others in the leadership team will have to shoulder the burden in different ways or drop some of the burden altogether and that, too, has high value. In the new churches, we protest loudly that we do not believe in one-man ministry. The reality is that in our practices we often err in that direction.

Some American universities have seen a similar issue in relation to academics and their usefulness in the technical or business world that they are intended to serve. So these universities have developed a novel plan. They only pay their professors 9 months salary and encourage each of them to go and work to: a) make a different contribution in a setting where the measurements are different; b) stay in touch with the realities of the world in which they play their academic part; and c) earn more than they could otherwise. There may be sound wisdom here and it may just be closer to the model of Paul we find in the Bible.

It works both ways

Let me relate two stories that illustrate the reality that this process can ebb and flow and work in both directions. A Baptist minister writes:

> I was reflecting the other day that I have now spent 38 years in one form or other of full-time employment. Right from leaving university, though I had no idea then what I wanted to do with my life, I had a strong sense of calling from God that my work would involve serving other people. I was chosen by Marks & Spencer for their management training scheme, and was very fulfilled there for the next 4 years.
>
> God then, as he often does, called me more specifically to work with young people through the vehicle of careers guidance. My previous work experience proved invaluable as, more and more, I took up leadership roles in the various organisations I worked for. Then 10 years ago, when I was beginning to contemplate a peaceful early retirement, God called again, this time into church pastoring. This in many ways was an extension of what I had been doing part-time for quite some time.
>
> This call to work for God's church was no different to the calls he had given me to work for Marks & Spencer and in the careers guidance field. I felt better prepared to do the work I am doing now through previous experience, but in no way was my calling any more significant than before.
>
> As a church pastor, I am in a better place to affirm the calling of God in the lives of others, especially in the workplace. I believe Christians must see the call of God as a recurring theme throughout their lives, and to rejoice in where God has placed them for that particular season, knowing that he may well call them to use their gifts as other opportunities present themselves.

Another friend has had his ebb and flow of calling move in the opposite direction. He writes:

> After many years in, what has become known as, 'full-time' ministry, I was out of a job when our church closed. We had already sensed that one of the purposes of the closure was to release the

members into the many gifts they had that could not be adequately expressed through what we then called 'church'. I had a one big question: 'What was I now to do?'

Previously, I had spent years working with young people, teaching and training, and my love of all things technical occasionally gave me opportunities to produce various kinds of audio and video media.

I trained as a personal development coach (which was in itself life-changing) and after 2 years I had a call from the wife of one of my best friends. We were being given the opportunity to develop a three-day training programme for sports coaches working with marginalised young people. If the pilot project worked well, we would have further opportunities. We quickly said yes, but there were a few challenges. We had to deliver the course in just 10 weeks and, as it was for the government, we had to quickly learn a whole new language and style.

We had a very intense few months but came up with the goods including training manuals and resource DVDs. I was able to build in personal development materials as well as material from a book I had previously written. We delivered the courses and got impressive feedback. I am so grateful to my friend and his wife and the ongoing plans of God which have helped me transition into a commercial environment.

Let's pray

I know that what I have written is not for all leaders, but I am convinced that it is for some, perhaps even many. If that is the case, please, 'test everything and hold on to what is good'. But please, don't be afraid of asking God to lead you to where he wants you to be. If your heart is beating a little faster, if there are one or two tears, if there is that wonderful moment right now where you know God is speaking, then ask him for a radical repackaging – whatever that means. Go on, be encouraged!

And for those of us in the workplace, while reading this chapter, could you pray and ask God how you could practically help, support and encourage those who are on your church staff?

Live Life

9.

Six Months Without Pay!

A friend of mine in British Columbia, Canada, worked as a director of a small exhibition centre there. It's a job he loved and one that suited his abilities to a tee. Unfortunately, a few years back, the federal government took the decision to cut off all funding to the programme, which meant that all the directors, including my friend, were laid off. Naturally this was a tough place to be, but it was made all the more challenging by the fact that my friend often used to say to people that 'we work for God and not for pay'. The question now running through his mind was whether he could live up to that conviction.

Having taken counsel from his father and some Christian friends he trusted, he decided to carry on doing his job without any guaranteed pay.

After one particularly difficult day and because he was no longer being officially employed, my friend decided to knock off early. As he was turning the key in the door, he sensed God saying to him, 'Why are you leaving early?' To which he responded 'Because I'm not getting paid!' There was a fleeting silence in which my friend felt he had given a justifiable answer – and then these words touched his spirit: 'Doesn't that depend on who you consider your employer to be?'

Needless to say, he went back to work and God provided for him and his family for a full 6 months until a federal government review not only reinstated all the funding but they gave my friend full back-pay with which he paid off his mortgage.

I love this story, but I also find it a challenge that gets right to the heart of what motives and reasons I have for doing the work I do.

What does the Bible say?

If I asked you to tell me why you work and to give me a biblical basis for your answer, I wonder, what would you say? I wonder, too, if that would be what you really believe. So what does the Bible say?

- Matt. 6:33: 'But seek first the kingdom of God and his righteousness, and all these things shall be added to you.'
- 2 Thes. 3:10–15: 'For even when we were with you, we commanded you this: If anyone will not work, neither shall he eat. For we hear that there are some who walk among you in a disorderly manner, not working at all, but are busybodies. Now those who are such we command and exhort through our Lord Jesus Christ that they work in quietness and eat their own bread. But as for you, brethren, do not grow weary in doing good. And if anyone does not obey our word in this epistle, note that person and do not keep company with him, that he may be ashamed. Yet do not count him as an enemy, but admonish him as a brother.'
- 1 Thes. 4:11,12: 'Aspire to lead a quiet life, to mind your own business, and to work with your own hands, as we commanded you, that you may walk properly toward those who are outside, and that you may lack nothing.'
- Col. 3:22—4:2: 'Bondservants, obey in all things your masters according to the flesh, not with eyeservice, as men-pleasers, but in sincerity of heart, fearing God. And whatever you do, do it heartily, as to the Lord and not to men, knowing that from the Lord you will receive the reward of the inheritance; for you serve the Lord Christ. But he who does wrong will be repaid for what he has done, and there is no partiality. Masters, give your bondservants what is just and fair, knowing that you also have a Master in heaven. Continue earnestly in prayer, being vigilant in it with thanksgiving.'
- Ecc. 2:24–26: 'Nothing is better for a man than that he should eat and drink, and that his soul should enjoy

good in his labour. This also, I saw, was from the hand of God. For who can eat, or who can have enjoyment, more than I? For God gives wisdom and knowledge and joy to a man who is good in his sight; but to the sinner he gives the work of gathering and collecting, that he may give to him who is good before God. This also is vanity and grasping for the wind.'

- Ecc. 5:19 'be happy in his work – this is a gift of God' (NIV).
- Prov. 22:29: 'Do you see a man who excels in his work? He will stand before kings; he will not stand before unknown men.'

A pure motive

We have begun to see a vision; what kind of people will it take to fulfil that vision? What kind of attitudes and motives are required? From these scriptures, as well as others we have already looked at, we can deduce some pure motives for our work.

1. 'Seek first the kingdom . . .' (Matt. 6:33). In these words, Jesus expressed the true motive – seek first the kingdom of God, and all these things will be added to you. Notice the key word – added – not taken. All things may indeed be added, but a pure motive is, 'I work where I do because I am called, led and directed by a working God, and it is my primary sphere, where I work out what it means to seek first the kingdom of God.'
2. I work because it is a fundamental instruction. 'If anyone will not work, neither shall he eat . . . if anyone does not obey our word in this epistle . . . work with your own hands, as we commanded you . . .' (2 Thes. 3:10–15). In other words, I should be so crystal clear that working is my minimum contribution to life on this earth that I hold no doubt about it. It is what I was created to do.
3. '. . . [A man should] be happy in his work'. I work because it is good for me. God has given it to me to enjoy. When

I work it gives meaning, pleasure and a wholesome out-let to express what God himself has placed within me. When I work there is joy because I am in the place of God's leading or choosing. I suspect that without that joy, we would not know that we were on the right track in the first place. The joy of the Lord is our strength – his joy in our use of our gifts.

4. I do it for Jesus, not for money, not for the church, not for anything other than God himself. 'And whatever you do, do it heartily, as to the Lord and not to men, know-ing that from the Lord you will receive the reward of the inheritance; for you serve the Lord Christ' (Col. 3:23,24). What a liberating concept! Even in the worst of all work-ing conditions, slavery, Paul says, 'You are doing it for Jesus, so do it with your whole heart – it is him you are serving.' I can't tell you the hundreds of times I have counselled men and women who tell me, 'We are des-perate to serve Jesus but simply don't know what his will is.' Friend, the will of God is in front of your hands and noses, go and do some work and work at it with all your heart and might. You can spend the whole of your life waiting to hear from God about how you can serve him, and miss it right in your own backyard.

Common misunderstandings

1. *I work to provide for my family*

This confuses some people. What about the scripture in 1 Tim. 5:8, which says, 'But if anyone does not provide for his own, and especially for those of his household, he has denied the faith and is worse than an unbeliever'? If we don't work, we should not eat! Sure, but that is the most extreme basic laid down for peo-ple trying to avoid work at all cost – it's not the *raison d'être* for positive, God-inspired work. Similarly, provision for my family is not the primary reason for working. Our true motivation should be that I am created for this, this is what God has placed me here to do and I am called by God to do it joyfully and wholeheartedly.

2. *I work to support myself so that I can do what's important at church*

This is an easy trap to fall into – it sounds like a good motive but in reality it's a denial of the work God has given us to do on a day-to-day basis. Not only that, our hearts will not be in our jobs, we will easily be de-motivated, distracted and unfulfilled making us poor employees – not a good witness for loving work and living life as God intended.

3. *I work to bring financial prosperity*

We don't work to prosper, that is not what drives us nor is it our primary aim. That doesn't mean I don't believe in profit, after all, as a businessman I need to be a good steward of what God has blessed me with for my sake and for the sake of those I am responsible for as an employer. But as a motive, well it hides a whole can of worms – chief of which is that I will never be truly satisfied, I will always be chasing more and more because no one ever feels rich enough when it comes to financial wealth. Remember, the love of money is the root of all kinds of evils.

4. *I work for status or career advancement*

I believe with all my heart in career advancement. I believe in Joseph, Daniel and Esther rising to the top of their environments. I believe in commitment and excellence providing a basis for that to happen. But, that is not to be our drive, or our motivation, for self-serving reasons. I believe in men and women at the top of every sphere of society serving God there. But that is the focus – serving God there, not status or career advancement there. The line between the two approaches may be a fine one, but it is surely there. And the heart knows, better than we do, how to hide that difference. If this is our motivation, then sooner or later selfishness will accelerate and pride will produce the normal crop of spiritual barrenness and dryness.

5. *I work to provide for the church*

Like the second error, this one can be so wonderfully camouflaged. I know the scriptures about generous giving and about storing treasure in heaven, but I do not work to provide for the church. I believe in responsible giving to support the work of the church, but as a reason for work it is another concealed deception. This motive often hides a secret love for money camouflaged by good intent. I have seen churches dependent on one or two wealthy individuals for finance – a risky strategy. I have spoken to many people who wanted to start a business to provide for the church, in the belief that God would bless such motives, only to see those businesses fail. If we get our motive right, then a fruit will certainly be our ability to give more – but as a motive for work, it's a poor one, fraught with pitfalls.

6. Full-time ministry

If our eyes, our heart and our thoughts are set on getting away from our current employment and into full-time church work, I will be robbing my business, my employer, my work colleagues of my full attention and energy. I will always be longing for something else, a future life at the expense of the present. I remember one manager who said to me, 'David, I need more staff but I don't want Christians because their commitment is not really wholehearted.' In 2 Chronicles it says, 'he sought the Lord and worked wholeheartedly and so he prospered.'

7. Working to get, not give

There is often a welfare mentality in our approach to work. That's why, for many, the thought of working without pay is very alien. If we are truly working for Jesus with a whole heart, then we will truly be working to give and not just to get. In my attitudes to reward, two key things should prevail – gratitude and contentment. The world's mould and pressure is a constant barrage of ingratitude, discontentment and demands. Materialism is wanting things now – that new kitchen, suite, clothes – now! God's way is to add these things – but on his timescale. If we lose gratitude it is easy to become obsessed with what I'm taking out, instead of focusing on what I'm putting in. When that happens the passion goes. The job itself may well be right but something has shifted in my motives.

If we can settle the issues in this chapter, some wonderful possibilities will flow from our work. We will discover that work is not solely for our own needs and satisfaction. We will discover that work enables us to give to those less fortunate than ourselves.

The *raison d'être* for work

Work is not there to provide big money for the church.
Work is not there to provide God with money that he is otherwise short of.
Work is not there to be 'tent making', to enable me to fulfil my ministry.
Work is not there for our prosperity.
Work is not there for our personal fulfilment.
Work is not there to train us for leadership.

Work may indeed provide some of these elements, but they are fruits, they are not the root or the *raison d'être*. The *raison d'être* is simply that God works and we are created in his image to do likewise. For most of us, we will express our destiny and calling of God primarily through work. If we will believe that then the dynamic of God's kingdom, the Holy Spirit, will be available for us to take God's kingdom into our work.

Work enables us to serve others and thereby contribute to the life of others. The way the Carpenter put it was 'to love others as you love yourself'. Work becomes the main sphere of life for the majority of us where we can actually work that out.

A checklist

Read through the following statements and tick the three which most accurately reflect what you really believe are your motives for working:

- I work primarily to provide for myself and my family.
- I work to earn enough to enable me to do my real work for God.
- I work to support others in the church.
- I work as a means to financial prosperity.

- I am working as a stop-gap until I sense God's calling on my life.
- I work because I have been created to do just that, and it is where I practically out-work 'seeking first the kingdom of God'.
- I work here because this is where God has called and led me to.
- I work in this occupation because it is the best outlet for me to put to work the gifts, skills and talents that God has given me.

Now rank those three in order of real importance to you (1, 2 and 3). How do your three choices line up with this chapter and what changes could you make?

10.

God's Anvil

I love to watch a blacksmith at work. I glimpse a quality of eternity in the fire and pressure being applied to unyielding, dirty-looking, raw iron. One thing is for sure, without that heat and the skill of the craftsman, the raw material is simply not going to change. Hammer it without heat and all you will do is dent it. Heat it without the hammer and all you have is hot potential. In Isaiah, God says, 'I created you, O Jacob, I formed you, O Israel.' The Hebrew for 'create' means 'producing out of nothing'. The Hebrew for 'forming' carries with it the idea of a process which changes shapes and moulds us.

When a Samurai sword is made, it is heated, hammered over and cooled down. Heated, hammered over, cooled down. It is that harsh repetitive process that gives it its unique strength and its ultimate sharpness. There is no other way to do it. Jas. 1:5 puts it like this: 'If any of you lacks wisdom, let him ask of God, who gives to all liberally and without reproach, and it will be given to him.' What does he give liberally? Look at verse 2 and you will find the answer – 'various trials'. Loads of them! Do you still want wisdom? The passage goes on to say, in verse 3, 'knowing that the testing of your faith produces patience'. Patience, or perseverance, must finish its work so that you may be complete or mature, not lacking anything.

The word 'testing' means proving and refers to the crucible. In Malachi, God's refiner's fire is written about. In Old Testament times, they would suspend gold in a crucible or melting pot over the hottest fire the refiner could produce. As the metal seethed in the pot, the 'dross' or impurities would force their way to the surface and be skimmed off. The process was repeated until all the impurities were removed. The refiner was not satisfied until he could see his own face clearly in the metal. Metals that passed the test of refining were accepted; metals that failed the test were rejected.

The Father's anvil for his Son

Jesus knew this crucible. Jesus knew this anvil process. The Bible says of him that 'he learnt obedience through the things he suffered.' I have heard it preached many times, but few have really suggested how this works in practice. Certainly one of the things I believe it means in practice, is that much of what he learned he would have learned from his working world. Jesus would have faced so many of the pressures that we face as working people. There was no secular barrier or line that he was afraid to cross. This is the Son of God. If it was so for him it can be even more so for us. Where did the strength of resolve to handle the Garden of Gethsemane come from? Because, in 18 years, he had learned through the anvil of work. The world of work was the Father's anvil for the Son that he loved, the Son who pleased him, the perfect Son.

I have seen this in a small way with my own children. We have done lots of memorable things together. We pioneered, with an organisation called High Force, Father and Son and Father and Daughter events which Care for the Family now run to provide marvellous, unforgettable experiences together. But the most memorable, the most life-changing events, have often come through the world of work. I remember videoing Joshua's last day on his paper round and sending a copy to his brother Joel. Why? Because that was Joshua's first job, which had been passed on to him by his brother. They had both spent 3 years learning obedience through the weather they suffered, the extra houses they delivered to and commitment when ill. I was proud of their achievement and content with what they had learned.

When we moved into our current home, the landscape gardener offered to pay Joel to move some huge rocks from the bottom of a very steep bank up to the garden itself. Joel came up to my office after 20 minutes, dispirited and lonely. 'No way am I going to move all that on my own!' he stated. I said nothing. He came back a few minutes later. 'Set your clock,' he said. 'I am going to do it in 2 hours, and I am going to do it for you.' Sure enough, it was done. At 13, Joel had learned one of the most powerful lessons imaginable about money, motivation and relationships at work. Where else could he have learned that?

Work is a marvellous mirror of reality. At work you can't rationalise or spiritualise failure or mistakes. You can't say, 'I'm sure my decision was the will of God,' when you just lost your employer £50,000 in a negotiation. Market research shows that the average employer is not overly impressed with Rom. 8:28 – preferring to call a failure a failure!

So for this reason and many others, work, in truth, is God's main tool to shape us into what we should be. That is not to say that character development is the *raison d'être* for work; it is, however, one of its fruits. Let's look at some of these areas.

Wisdom

If we embrace the mistakes, admonishments, correction and successes in our God-filtered, God-ordered working environment, then inevitably we will become wiser. Again, we tend to think of wisdom as related to the spiritual realm – church, Bible, meetings. Many of us have been rightly taught that the fear of God is the beginning of wisdom but Proverbs also tells us, that 'wisdom cries out in streets and in city gateways' – the place of commerce. Jesus described the sons of this age learning wisdom from the real world of work.

Ruling

Many of us will have been taught that the kingdom of God involves us ruling, or taking responsibility for, the sphere in which God has placed us. Along with the family, work is a prime area to learn how to rule yourself, how to rule in the sphere where God places you and, where appropriate, how to rule others. We are all tempted to bring selfishness, misery, poverty, repression, lack of discipline, lack of government and all kinds of fear and resentments into our workplace. But, with God's help, we can bring redemption to that sphere which God gives us. We can open the door for the kingdom of God to impact our work.

Joseph ultimately ruled a nation very successfully and this had much to do with his skill development through work. Think of his path – from dream to pit, to Potiphar, to prison, to prime minister. Where did he learn to hone his wisdom? Where did he learn his administrative skills? On the anvil of work.

Daniel, as a teenager, became a prisoner of war. Taken hundreds of miles away, forced to change his name and positioned in such a way that he would never see his family again. Through the years, Daniel not only survived the Babylonian rule, but eventually came to govern a third of the kingdom. He was known as a man with extraordinary spirit. But where did he learn to become a man of extraordinary spirit? On the anvil of work.

One of the great areas of ruling is patience. This tests me to the hilt, and never more than when Joel came home after 2 years away and set up his office close to mine. I have preached the 'father and son' model for years and longed for the day when one of my kids would put it into practice. I was busy revising my theology after the first day! Joel likes to interrupt – I mean not just once a day, but let's say once or twice every 30 minutes. That, dear mathematical reader, is up to four times each hour – a staggering thirty-two interruptions per day!

After the first few days, I was getting vexed and it showed because there was a very quiet appearance at my office door and when I looked up there was no one there. However, stuck to my door with BluTack, was the following quotation: 'Interruptions can be viewed as sources of irritation or opportunities for service, as moments lost or experience gained, as time wasted or horizons widened. They can annoy us or enrich us, get under our skin or give us a shot in the arm, monopolise our minutes or spice our schedules, depending on our attitude toward them.'

I had been got! But that's the nature of the anvil.

Reputation

The qualifications for elders and deacons in the books of Timothy and Titus are based on character rather than ministry. In fact, if you count them you will find thirty-three character-related and just one ministry-related statements. Where are we going to find a reputation like that, particularly with outsiders?

We know that ministry flows out of what we are. We can never minister what we are not, or what we don't have. We can act it. But we cannot minister it. Leadership in the Body of Christ should be a reflection of what you are at work. Work is not there to pay for you to be a leader. Work is not there to make you a leader. Work, as we have said, is there as God's calling for our lives, the fruit of which will be a man or woman who can be called and anointed of God to minister to others in the church. Many great men and women of God have learned how to rule, lead or govern through the world of work, e.g. William Wilberforce (politics), the Rowntree, Cadbury and Fry families (chocolate manufacturers), the Barclay family (banking).

Faith

For so many obvious reasons, the place of work is the place of faith development. I have clients who call me from time-to-time to ask me to pray for their sales that month. I had a client email and ask me to pray for one of his assignments, because an advert had unexpectedly bombed and he was at a loss for what to do. Why would they do that? Because they understand that a seamless God is interested in the month's sales figures and the anxiety over work done that has not yet been successful.

Most of the business ventures I have undertaken have been steps, sometimes leaps, of faith. What does that mean in practice? In reality, it means that I didn't have all the resources or skills necessary for the successful implementation of the project. It means that I approached it with apprehension. It also means that I believed I had heard God and my confidence would be in that word.

Everyone who is growing in faith will frequently be pushed or pulled into circumstances where more faith is needed. And, by its very nature, faith insists that I operate beyond the realms of the known into the unknown.

Have you noticed the biblical emphasis, live by faith. Normal Christian life will regularly and increasingly become full of faith.

Faith for every day – faith for every area. Faith, faith, faith. Faith is not occasional, not just for significant critical moments in life, but daily life. If we are not increasingly living by faith, then something is wrong.

Living by faith does not mean, in biblical terms, that you are a church-paid worker. The truth is some church-paid Christian workers talk about living by faith when they mean their salary is paid by the church, and in fact they may exercise very little real faith at all. Faith is for every Christian in every sphere of life, for every day, for every part of our life. To live as a Christian can only be real, meaningful dynamite when we live by faith, as we learn to bring every area of our life under the lordship of Jesus. So we need to bring every area of our life under faith. In Romans, we learn that the businessman Abraham is 'the father of all those who walk in the footsteps of the faith'. Galatians says, 'Since we live by the Spirit let us keep in step with the Spirit' (or 'let us walk with the Spirit'). God is so practical, so helpful – here he brings living in faith down to manageable steps, literally footsteps. Faith and the Spirit are inseparable – to walk in the footsteps of the faith is the same as walking in the footsteps of the Holy Spirit. Keeping in step with the Spirit is the same as walking, or keeping in step, with faith.

What does this mean in practice? Simply that, like many other great truths, we apply them in daily chunks – learning what it means to walk in faith. Taking one step after another it's easy, it's manageable, it's possible, it's for you and me. We hear God and do it in faith. We can apply this to software bugs, to difficult patients, to late payments, to business development, to shop floor difficulties and to problem relationships – faith.

Every leader you ever work with will fail in some way or other, and often God will allow hurt in these relationships. Why? Because on the anvil God wants, and needs, to be sure that your faith is in him and his Word and not in people or organisations. When we reach out in faith, God is not far away, not locked in heaven but God's power is there in our hearts and mouths waiting to be received.

Work is likely to be the place where we will need to hear God the most, it's where we spend the bulk of our time and face the majority of our biggest issues. If we are tuned in, if we are properly founded, if we are genuinely motivated, we can expect to hear God the most.

God's anvil is where character is hammered out, destiny is unlocked, faith is released and where our seamless ministry comes into its fullness.

11.

Money

I have asked one certain question all over the world: 'Do you believe that money is the root of all evil?' I well remember one occasion when I was asking this question of leaders and a congregation in a wooden building on the outskirts of Harare, Zimbabwe. Most of the congregation kept their hands down and looked at me smugly, as if to say, 'OK, preacher, we have got your number, nice try, but we're not falling for that one!' And, as most of you know, they were right – it is one of the most commonly misquoted scriptures ever! It is the *love* of money that is the root of all kinds of evil and not the money itself.

In the laughter and fun that followed, I asked them another question: 'How many of you here would like to be rich?' This time, just about everyone's hand went up, including most if not all of the leaders! In fact, I have asked this question scores of times, and around 80 per cent of the average audience – leaders included – put up their hands. Let me tell you what I told my friends in Harare that morning. Those of you that raised your hands are on a six-step slide to destruction. They looked at me, hoping I was winding them up. But I wasn't, because I had in my mind Paul's words to Timothy about riches expressed in 1 Tim. 6: 9–10 *'People who want to get rich fall into'* the six steps below:

Riches:
1. cause you to fall into temptation and a trap
2. make you have foolish and harmful desires
3. plunge people into ruin and destruction

4. if you love them, are the root of all kinds of evil
5. have caused some people eager for money to wander from the faith
6. can make you pierce yourself with many griefs

A true story

I want to tell you a true story from another country. I knew a para-church organisation whose leader had chosen his workers carefully. Every one of them had a strong professed love for the Lord, and they worked well as a ministry team together. They had occasional differences – but seemed to work through them quite well.

One of the workers was given the responsibility of the cheque book, banking and petty cash. He kept good accounts, but he often rocked the boat a bit and had bouts of anger and aggression towards his fellow workers and even the leader. One night, during an outreach meal, someone gave a very costly present to the leader as a 'thank you'. The treasurer was furious. 'What a waste of money,' he said. 'Why don't we sell the thing and put the money towards our outreach programme for the poor?' Unable to let this matter rest, a few days later he phoned up the secret police, who had been taking an interest in what they saw as a subversive group of people. He informed on the leader and took a large amount of money for his trouble. The leader was arrested and suffered such terrible torture, he died. When he heard the news the treasurer deeply regretted what he had done and what he had become. He took back the money and was never seen or heard of again.

The leader was well known to most of you – his name was Jesus. Judas was the treasurer. Here what's really concerning about this story. Outwardly, Judas was a good disciple. He had genuine faith, genuine relationships and genuine gifts from God. He was a good businessman with some very strong principles and moral standpoints. But he had a secret love and that love was money.

In John's Gospel, we discover that he used to take money – literally sneak it from God's pocket! How could he do that? Because he had a love for money that he kept hidden. The other disciples had their flaws, their mistakes, but they were open. Peter, James and John were open, faced up to their flaws and weaknesses and allowed Jesus to teach them a better way. But Judas' love of money was so well hidden that no one knew for three years. In that secrecy, his desire grew worse, eventually plunging him into ruin and destruction.

Judas was seduced by money and fell in love with it, and as he got eager for it he lost his faith and finally took another person's life and then his own. If he could have opened up and shared his weakness, if he had cried for help and repented, he could so easily have been saved. James makes it clear: 'Confess your trespasses to one another, and pray for one another, that you may be healed.'

Looking in the mirror

Jesus once said that we need to remove the planks from our own eye before we seek the specks of dust from other people's. To do that, we need to be willing to take a long hard look at our lives to make sure we aren't captivated by the same sorts of desires that proved to be Judas' downfall.

Ask yourself this tough question: Do any of the following apply to me?

1. Do you believe that godliness is a means to financial prosperity?
2. Do you give, so that you can get.
3. Do you find it difficult to give often, readily, cheerfully and sacrificially.
4. Are you motivated in your work by the money you get from it?
5. Are you stealing from your employer – not just resources   that you think are trivial, but time? Are you abusing your   privileges and position?
6. Are you hiding any areas of finance that need confessing?
7. Are you lying about your finances?

Such problems aren't new. They are not just the result of our commercially driven, consumerist society. The New Testament church had its fair share of problems with money and the detrimental affects it had on those who fell in love with it – most notably the shocking story of Ananias and Sapphira. Why? Because Peter had had enough of disciples who lied about their finances. Isn't it interesting that the problem area for Judas and the problem area for Ananias and Sapphira was money? I think the lessons we need to learn are to be truthful, honest, easy to correct and self-revealing when it comes to money.

I had a fascinating experience some years back. During my devotional time one morning, I felt God say quite clearly that I was to set a limit on my earnings and give half of the rest away into ministry of one kind or another. I wrote it down in my prayer diary and set up an Excel spreadsheet to do the calculations. It all seemed OK but I noticed a change in my attitude. I no longer had any motivation to work – it all seemed such a drudge. I found anger surfacing in me every time I did the spreadsheet calculations. What was going on? God was revealing a hidden motivator and it was money! When I couldn't get all that I was earning, it took away the impetus to earn and my real motives were exposed.

Blessed to bless others

'Blessing' simply means 'more of what you have got that is good'. That includes both the material and spiritual. Listen to these words taken from God's directives to the people of Israel:

> I will bless you in all your work and in everything you put your hands to.

> The Lord your God will bless you in all your harvest and in all the work of your hands and your joy will be complete.

> The Lord your God will make you prosper.

Interestingly, in each of these cases, the blessing was not for self-indulgence – it was a reward for 'faith in action', as the Israelites did things for one another, and for God, that made no financial sense. These things included lending freely, cancelling debts and spending 3 weeks a year dedicated to appearing before God with no work being done. Whatever else the prospering of the Israelites entailed, it was not primarily for self-consumption.

Financial gain is not the goal of our service to God nor of our obedience in following him to the workplace of his choice. If it is the goal or faith objective of our working life we will be robbed, and whether we have financial gain or not, we will be robbed of truth.

How to be really prosperous

Prosperity in the Bible is both spiritual and financial. Prosperity means the well-being of spirit and soul as well as money, goods, food and possessions. It is not the same as materialism. Materialism says, 'I want more, I want more now, I want what they have got, I want what I cannot afford.' Religious materialism says, 'I will be godly and apply the rules of the Bible in order that I may be prosperous.' The outcome of that may or may not be a fact, but the motive is impure. James makes that clear when he says, 'You ask and do not receive, because you ask amiss, that you may spend it on your pleasures.' As we saw in an earlier chapter, if we seek first the kingdom, all these things will be added. Remember the mathematical term 'added'. Not multiplied. It implies a process, line upon line, little on little. Proverbs even says, 'he who gathers money little by little makes it grow'. Prosperity is seen as a process. Prosperity is also for the soul and includes well-being, whereas materialism is the pursuit of possessions. So we can expect godly prosperity to carry with it the ability to enjoy with peace what God has to give. It is widely suggested that the writer of Ecclesiastes was depressed or disillusioned and expressing that somewhat negative season in his writings. Isn't it interesting that even in that context, workplace wisdom resonates positively? The writer puts it like this: 'As for every man to whom God has given riches and wealth, and given him power to eat of it, to receive his heritage and rejoice in his labour – this is the gift of God.'

So we could define prosperity as something not to be pursued, but as something which God adds, rather than something we take. And prosperity includes the gift of God to enjoy what we have. If we are kept in a constant place of need, then we need to check our attitude – God may be keeping us there for a reason.

Stewarding our prosperity

Prosperity is for stewardship, not for self-consumption. That is not to say that possessions are intrinsically wrong or un-spiritual. Nor does it mean we have to adopt a lifestyle of poverty. Jesus had no place of his own, yet he had a coat of value that was gambled for because of its quality. He had no problem receiving an anointing of perfumed lotion costing thousands in today's value. He could also say, 'You cannot be my disciple if you don't give up every thing you have.' And he could say to the rich young ruler, 'Sell all you have and follow me.' That is not contradiction, it is truth in tension. What we own, and are blessed with, is there for us to steward – for our lives, for our families, for the poor and for the kingdom of God.

Our family has known times of great financial hardship and times of plenty. The challenges of both are different, but the reality of God and his presence are the same in both. I can remember Gill sitting on the stairs crying because we did not have enough money to buy shoes for our children. I have seen joy in her eyes – deep joy – when we have been able to give into different situations and make a difference with that giving. God has been in both.

I know a number of successful men and women who feel the need to justify their wealth, by implying that the reason they are running a business is so that they can fund a specific project or church or whatever. That is a wonderful out-working of stewardship, maybe, but it is not why they are working. As we saw before, it is fruit, not root.

In the church world that I am involved with, there is one particular businessman who has invested time and time again into projects large and small that the national leaders have set up. This man is a godly man and has among other things owned

some huge DIY retail outlets. But his reason for running businesses was not to fund church projects; his reasons were to do
with the call of God and the skills and talents he has. The giving
is a fruit not a motivation. If you read Hudson Taylor's biography
in two volumes, the role of one prominent businessman often
crops up. Without him, Taylor would not have done all that he
did. But this man did not go into business in order to finance
Taylor – it was the fruit of his stewardship. Why the emphasis on
a seemingly minimal distinction? Because that distinction affects
motives and it affects the desire, or need, to have control and
those can become very big and very damaging issues in the Body
of Christ.

12.

Let's Talk About Sex

You might be forgiven for asking why there is a chapter on sex in a book about work! Well the answer is simple – when men and women work together in a close environment their minds are not always on the task at hand. Work is one of the most common places for affairs to start, and it's easy to see why. Most people, especially those who work full time, spend more time with their colleagues than they do with their partners. It's not surprising, therefore, that many working people forge close friendships, often becoming emotionally vulnerable, confiding in colleagues, looking to them for support, especially if things aren't going well at home. Indeed, some working relationships are so close and intense, it's not hard to see why temptations to take things beyond the boundaries of an appropriate and professional relationship are more common than we'd like to imagine. In fact, time and time again, if there is one subject that people want to broach with me in private conversations, correspondence and at seminars and conferences, it's problems with sexual temptation at work. This is a major problem for working men and women, with the sobering truth that any one of us can be tempted because we are all human. Yet, despite all this, very few Christian working men and women, or their churches, talk openly enough about it – and sexual temptation thrives on silence. So let's talk about sex!

Sex is beautiful

Whenever I speak about work I always try to talk about sex and sexual temptation as much as possible. Not because I am particularly obsessed with the issue, but because there has been a reluctance to talk about the subject among Christians and difficulty in broaching the topic without embarrassment. When I do speak openly about sex and relationships, on nearly every occasion, men and women have come to me afterwards, or later on, and confessed some difficulty with sexual temptation in one form or another.

Sexual activity is not hidden in Scripture, it is not taboo nor is it regarded as embarrassing or smutty. The act of lovemaking is a God-given pleasure for humans to enjoy. The Bible does not hide its comments, positive or negative – it is plain. It also spells out unequivocally what the boundaries are, and what the consequences are of crossing those boundaries.

The Scriptures are full of instructions, guidelines, promises, warnings, consequences and blessings, all related to sex. Song of Solomon – whatever its alternative theological significance – is erotic poetry at its finest. What a loving God, who includes, at the very heart of Scripture, poetry that can raise the act of physical love to a height where it can be included in inspired writing. That fact alone, with no other evidence, would lead us to understand that God views human lovemaking as an inspired part of his creation, something clean and pure enough to include in his handbook for his creation. Equally, the book of Proverbs talks freely about intimacy, and in describing ways to avoid immorality, encourages us to find fulfilment in the context of marriage.

Dealing with sexual temptation

The first thing to say is that we mustn't think of sexual temptation in and of itself as something immoral. Being tempted isn't the problem, after all, we are all tempted in all kinds of ways everyday of our lives. The issue is how we respond to sexual temptation. Therefore, we need equipping to deal with temptation when it comes our way.

Three misconceptions about temptation:

Temptation is sin. Actually, the Bible portrays temptation as a process that 'assesses' what is within us. It's a test of our character and helps us to understand our moral boundaries and commitments. One of the Greek words used in the Bible, *peiras-mod*, means 'trials or testing with a beneficial purpose and effect'. Therefore, we don't need to view temptation negatively or with fear. Temptation is testing designed to bring out what is really there in our hearts, as part of the process of maturing. Temptation is not a sin. The understanding of this is fundamental to dealing with temptations that come our way. So many Christians experience guilt and condemnation when we are tempted sexually. But it's how we handle temptation that will determine the outcome. As the writer of the letter to the Hebrews makes clear; Jesus was tempted in every way just as we are – yet was without sin.

It's only me! I'm the only one bad enough to have this sexual temptation. I must be very bad, very un-spiritual – no one else in this church has this weakness. Don't you believe it! 1 Corinthians says, 'No temptation has seized you except what is common to all.' Every temptation, the seemingly innocuous to the obviously wicked, is experienced by other men and women. If you are tempted, remind yourself how very normal you are.

I can't cope! Oh, yes you can! God promises that you can. God is faithful and will not let you be tested beyond what you can bear. But when you are tempted, he will also provide a way out so that you can stand up under it.

Essential keys for handling sexual temptation

1. *Be open*
This means we determine from now on that we will not hide our problems or temptations. Hiding is an enemy in itself. One of the biggest problems we face in dealing with sexual temptation is the belief that it is simply too shameful to share. I want to see this reversed so that we believe it is shameful not to share and very normal and natural to share.

'Open' also means that, as a fundamental prerequisite, we have settled the issue that we cannot handle temptation on our own. Jesus did not teach us to pray, 'Lead me not into temptation.' No, Jesus said, 'Lead us not into temptation' and also 'Confess your faults one to another and pray for one another'. Temptation is not meant to be handled on our own. If you have a regular temptation or habit that is troubling you, in many cases you will not break it until you share it. It is not failure or weakness to need help, it is part of the humbling knowledge that we cannot cope in our own strength.

2. *Be honest*

This means what it says. When we confess our temptation or sins, we tell it like it is. I was once staying alone in a guest house in a remote part of Sweden. I had been away for some days and that evening, after finishing my consultancy with a nearby company, I sat down for my meal. The meal was superb, the place itself very romantic and I was totally on my own. There were no other guests and no other diners. The waitress, an extremely beautiful woman, came over and slowly handed me the menu, keeping her eyes on me and keeping her hand on the menu in such a way that it would touch mine. As soon as our hands touched, I knew something was happening but even so my reaction was not immediate. My hand stayed there for a few seconds and the feeling was pleasant. Nothing like that had ever happened to me before – it had taken me by surprise. I struggled with guilt for the rest of that meal and for some time after. When I came to share the situation with another Christian leader, I found an inner reluctance to be really honest. I could have fudged it. One part of me wanted to tell him a half-truth, something like, 'I was put into an awkward situation where a pretty waitress was looking suggestively at me.' Why the inner struggle to talk about the fact that our hands had touched? I am not absolutely sure, but I know that if I had not got the honest facts out, the same thing could have happened again. Honesty defeats that particular sin for the moment and puts stronger moral fibre within, to prevent anything similar happening again.

3. *Be self-revealing*

This means we go out of our way to detail the truth, rather than waiting for it to be dug out. Over the years, I have observed that people with habitual sexual sin find it very difficult to be self-revealing. The reason is often that they don't actually want to give up that sin, and the lack of self-revelation is a symptom of a hardened or fearful heart that does not want to give too much away. Self-revelation means we reveal the detail quickly so that the sinful acts – like an uprooted weed exposed to the sunlight – rapidly wither away.

4. *Set yourself some ground rules*
You know where your danger areas lie. I have one friend who was so tempted by hotel videos that he would take a screwdriver with him to dismantle the VCR's plug and then call one of us to confirm that he had done just that. It may seem extreme, but it worked. We have tried over the years to make sure that no married men travel on their own with just one woman in a car.

My wife and I live 12 miles from our church. Difficult and restricting as it may be, neither my wife nor I will make such a journey alone with a member of the opposite sex if it is at all possible. If it's not possible to avoid this situation we simply have open communication so that everyone knows who is going where, with who and when.

5. *Know your triggers and take responsibility for them*
What are your triggers? Alcohol? Alcohol will always lower our moral guard, so be aware of how much you are drinking and in what setting. Loneliness, tiredness and particular colleagues at work can also be triggers. Success at work or in some church-related programme can often lower our guard. We all have different triggers that make us vulnerable to temptation, so try and avoid these at all cost.

6. *Keep the door open*
Never have a closed door in your house or office when you are on the Internet. Never shut the door when you are counselling or alone with someone of the opposite sex. My kids over the years found this boundary easy to follow and would very comfortably challenge me if they thought I was in my office on the Net with the door closed.

7. *Define it and deal with it*

When temptation comes, recognise it and then remind yourself what God has to say about it and then put it from your mind.

'This is adultery. It is sin – "Do not commit adultery".'

'This is lust. It is sin – "Do not go after the lust of your eyes and your heart".'

8. *Pray*

Last, but certainly not least, pray about sexual temptations. The Lord's prayer says: 'Lead us not into temptation, but deliver us from evil.' These are not idle words but life-changing truths. When I pray, temptation feels perceptibly lower. In Matthew, Jesus says, 'Watch and pray so that you will not fall into temptation'. The spirit is willing, but the flesh is weak – prayer strengthens both.

Can I ask you with all of my heart to resolve to go and share with others you trust, to be open, to be honest, to be self-revealing and above all to pray when you are tempted? I have watched hundreds of men and women do this over the years. They haven't been rejected, they haven't been treated with shame and contempt – they have been loved and encouraged back to full spiritual health and I thank God everyday for this practical demonstration of God's love being shown among his people.

13.

God at Work!

The music is pumping its sensual rhythm. Staff from my clients' companies are already dancing on the dance floor. I am sitting at a crowded table waiting for my first course. A very drunk man is sitting on my left and straight ahead is a Danish lady, whom I shall call Maria. I am sitting there and, in the deafening racket of that darkened room, with a boring conversation about marketing going on next to me, I am crying out to God to speak or do something. And then God begins to speak about the lady opposite, about the tears she has cried for one of her children, about how pleased he is with her care of her child and how he understands her pain.

With a fair bit of nervousness, I begin to relate all this to her. She begins to cry and says, 'I can't do this! I can't do this!' 'Can't do what?' I ask. 'I cannot cry,' she replies. 'I've built up a reputation at work for being tough. They must not see me cry.' Maria dashes off to the restroom and returns with her face freshly powdered. I talk to her for a little while and offer to pray for her son. She grabs at the offer and takes our home address so that she can call or email if there are any new developments.

I love those moments. I always feel inadequate, I usually doubt what I sense God is saying, but God is always faithful in bringing about a positive result. There is something wonderful in being part of God at work.

How do we work with God in our workplace?

Of all the issues covered in this book, this one probably vexes me the most. So far we have talked about a number of ways in which God works in all kinds of different facets of working life. But, ultimately, God's business will always be about people and I long to see more of God's kingdom touching people in the workplace.

We have counselled, taught or worked with thousands of people over the last decade or so. Throughout that time it has been rare to see real evidence of a powerful dynamic demonstration of God in a workplace setting. Acts says, 'but you shall receive power when the Holy Spirit has come upon you – and you shall be witnesses to me . . .' But where is the dynamic witness at work? Where is this power of God's kingdom at work?

1. We need an unshakeable belief that we are called to do our work

Why is this important?

i   More than half our waking hours are usually spent at work. The balance of our time is divided between family, church and other ministry.

ii Many people have doubts about the leading or calling of God and therefore never have a whole heart towards their work. I have already alluded to the fact that there are good business people who won't hire Christians because they know that the person's heart is not with them. Christians don't always make the best employees because of particular religious attitudes which rob the employer of their heart.

iii If God has called me here, if this is his choice of work for me, I can expect him to be with me in this work through the Holy Spirit.

2. Being clear about my root motives in my job

Jesus expressed it as, 'Seek first the kingdom of God and all these things shall be added unto you.' In work, our daily motive should be that God has called me here and this is where I will interface, or introduce, the kingdom of God into my little part of the world. If my root motives are money and career status, I will not seek first the kingdom and I am likely to be so preoccupied with my expectations and concerns that I miss the opportunities that are there to work with God.

3. Expectancy

If we know we are called of God and if our motives are pure, then we can legitimately expect God to move, and our faith and expectation levels can grow. I have been shocked at the number of people over the years who do not believe that God wants to work in their workplace. We should pray and expect God to be with us at our desks, in the classroom, on the shop floor, in the surgery, at the wheel. If we could really grasp his immanence – the reality of his presence – daily, intimately, genuinely, it would help us to be reassured that he values our work and that he wants us to be an important part in bringing the kingdom of God to our workplace.

God's view is, 'Never will I leave you, never will I forsake you.' So we can say with confidence that 'the Lord is my helper'. Can we grasp that, please? 'Never' means never! 'Never' includes the office argument, the dying patient, the board room confrontation, the mundane assembly line, or the frustrating commute.

My friend Mark Greene taught me to ask the question, 'Where is God when you are at work?'

4. We have to sow before we can reap

Harnessing the power of God in my life requires sowing before reaping. It begins on one level – with us, not God. Will I sow my seed for this life, this day, this family, this year, this house, this career, this business? Can I find a way to sow my life into things that have lasting and permanent value?

The sowing of seed is a picture used right through the Scriptures and Jesus used the concept for one of his most famous parables. The sowing of seed would be a poignant, powerful picture because everyday people were well aware that their future depended on enough seed being sown in the right place and at the right time.

What we are in God next week, next year and next decade will depend on what we sow today.

What does it mean to sow?

When we sow seeds in our garden, we take the seed, pop it underground and water it. Though sometimes we may forget about it, we expect that the life in it will cause it to grow in its proper time and produce beauty, shape, food, or whatever it's supposed to produce.

When we sow the seed of our life, we do it in four basic ways:

1. We sow with our mind – what we allow our thoughts to do.
2. We sow with our activity – what we do with our time.
3. We sow with our words – what we say.
4. We sow with our resources – our money, homes, possessions etc.

To summarise – sowing is what we do with our minds, our words, our activity and our resources (what we put ourselves and our possessions into). Sowing gives us the correct perspective – we're not going to produce miraculous or spectacular harvests overnight. Normally it takes time! What sometimes happens is that we pray into an area and lose heart because of apparent delays. We're impatient!

Some practical applications

1. Doing good
'Let us not become weary of doing good . . .'

I remember queuing in a works canteen. There were three or four Christians in the line. A lady was walking back to her table and slipped with her tray, spilling food and shattered glass all over the floor. One of the Christians, without even thinking, cleared up the mess. The lady was overcome by the kindness and it opened up several ongoing conversations. It also made an impact on another employee, who later brought his whole family into the church, was converted and finally baptised.

Doing acts of kindness could be as simple as a word of encouragement, taking some of another person's work and adding it to yours. Doing unusual things where the usual is expected. Let me tell you a true story which shows how the little things in a relationship can make a huge difference and you will see that any one of us, in any job, at any level can make a difference.

David worked in Sainsbury's. His dad would take him there and back when he could, partly because David had Down's syndrome. David's job was at the end of the till packing the bags for the shoppers. One night he went home and said to his dad, 'Dad, I want to find a way to thank everyone who comes to Sainsbury's to do their shopping.'

Wisely his father asked, 'How do you think you could do that, son?'

'I think I would like to write a letter,' said David.

So that night, David and his dad drafted a small note which said among other things, 'Thanks for choosing to come to Sainsbury's for your shopping, signed by David who packed your bag.' Every time he put shopping into a bag, David would drop the little note in.

A few days later, the store manager was walking the floor when he saw a long queue at one till, what puzzled him was that all the other tills were quiet. He wanted to find out what was going on so he asked each shopper in the queue why they were in that line when the other tills were quiet. The answer was the same from each shopper, 'We want David to pack our bags.' Even when packing plastic bags with shopping, a small relational act can touch the hearts of hardened shoppers.

2. Recognising the needs around us
Julian Sayer from Responsive Marketing writes:

> When I began working in the computer industry, it was very easy, at times, to kid myself that those around me were in little need of help. The external appearance was one of sophistication, confidence and determination to succeed. Over the years, however, I have had the opportunity to talk with, and pray for, people facing issues such as divorce, cancer in the family, a friend in a coma, office back-stabbing, psychological problems and abortion.

Each of these people have approached me, wanting to talk and knowing that I was a Christian. God will often use a natural friendship that has developed at work. However, some of these people have been those who I would not naturally have spent time with outside the office environment and others have been those whom I have not considered to be good at their jobs! The point I am making is that God will often break down barriers we have created in order to reach someone.

3. Loving and serving our neighbour

Recognising that there are well-concealed needs among those we work with is not enough. As I have mentioned, people will come to us on occasion, but this does not mean that we should sit back and wait, in the hope that a queue will soon form at our desk!

Jesus consistently took the initiative. He went to people he knew had need. He really loved and cared for people and we need to really love and care for people, too.

4. Love in action

Examples of opportunities to love and serve people, that are within the capabilities of most of us, are as follows:

- A 'thank you' note
- An apology for an inappropriate remark
- A word of encouragement
- Cards on special occasions
- Information spotted on someone's hobby
- Buying someone's sandwiches for them
- Taking an interest in people's families
- Making the tea for the team/department

Lorraine had worked for the team for over 2 years. Most of the team were Christians although most of the company, including Lorraine, were not!

Lorraine was on a low wage (certainly compared to the rest of us) and struggled to make it stretch each month, especially as she liked to party! One morning, she called the office to say she wouldn't be in as her car had broken down yet again. Before she knew what was happening, two of us appeared on her doorstep, took her to work, delivered her car to a garage and by 5:30 p.m. they were reunited.

Lorraine was close to tears as she suddenly realised that each member of the team had demonstrated their love for her by contributing to having her car repaired. This one act spoke more to her than anything we had said previously when we were sharing our faith with her.

People can ignore almost every direct communication of the gospel, but they cannot ignore us loving them! John sums this up with the simple but effective encouragement, 'Dear children, let us not love with words or tongue but with actions and in truth.'

5. Praying

I was running a marketing seminar in the Hilton Hotel in Basingstoke, for the Marketing Guild. As is my normal custom, I was shaking hands with delegates before the start and asking what they were looking for in particular. I had nearly finished the fifty or so delegates, when I came to one of the last, sitting right in the front close to my lectern. I said to him, 'What are you hoping to gain from today – why have you come?' He replied, 'I have come today to discover my destiny.' I was more than a bit surprised, so I said the first thing that entered my mind – food! I asked, 'How about we talk over a snack at lunch?' 'Fine,' he said.

Lunchtime came, the delegates left and this man and I were left alone in the room. He began to tell me that he had a broken marriage among other issues he was trying to deal with. It was one of those stories that leave you feeling totally inadequate. So I asked him the only thing I could think of: 'Would you like me to pray for you?'

'I would really like that,' he said.

'What would you like me to pray for?'

'I would like you to pray that I would discover my destiny,' he said.

As we prayed, a tear or two formed in his eyes. 'That was wonderful,' he said. 'Would you pray again?'

'Sure,' I said. 'What shall I pray this time?'

'Please pray that God would make himself real to me.'

This time the tear or two were in my eyes.

6. Just being

This is a story from Phillip Denning – a salesman:

> With each appointment that I go to, I make a point of always spending a few minutes in prayer beforehand, praying specifically for the person that I am visiting. I pray simply that, whatever the outcome, I will in some way be a blessing to the individual and to their company, and that in some way, no matter how small, they will be better off for having met me.
>
> Over the last few years, God has given me numerous opportunities to share the gospel with non-Christians, and to have fellowship with and encourage Christians also in the business world.
>
> Just over two years ago, I met with an engineer who had showed an interest in our company. We got on well, despite the fact that he was probably the crudest man that I have ever met! After about 6 months, he decided to place some business with me, and informed me that the reason that he knew we were 'kosher' was because he had seen my Bible in my car! Until that point I hadn't even mentioned to him that I was a Christian.
>
> A year later, I was visiting another company local to him, and I really felt that the Holy Spirit was prompting me to call in and see him again. However, as I was in a rush, and didn't want to get held up, I didn't go. Later in the day, he rang me out of the blue! 'I am ringing to say "Goodbye",' he told me. He then went on to say how his business was going under and how his wife had found out about the string of affairs that he had been having and had tried to kill him on two occasions by stabbing him! He had now decided to end his life, and was ringing me in a last attempt to find some hope, as he had remembered that I was a Christian. Thank God that he did. That was 6 months ago, he is still alive and he is regularly meeting with his local vicar!

14.

Working at Prayer

The hotel 'Le Beau Rivage' is situated in one of the most breath-takingly beautiful Alpine areas of the world. I had been conducting a marketing review there for a Swedish company, and in the process I became very close friends with Kiell Tofters and his wife Gertrude. Kiell was the marketing director and, in the first meeting, our mutual faith had emerged and caused a strong bond to develop. At the end of the day together, Kiell, Gertrude, a consultant friend of mine – Kees Rosies – and I stood in the moonlight overlooking the beautiful Lake Leman, and on its shores we began to pray. We prayed about Sweden, about destiny and about what God might have in mind for our newly-formed friendships.

Ten years later, I had the privilege of praying for elders to be inducted at the church where Kiell became the senior pastor. During those 10 years, God answered the prayers of that night. That contact led to the founding of my own business. It opened up a relationship between us which led to ongoing visits to Kiell's church. And, in the process, Kiell has been able to reach out to hundreds of other leaders in the Swedish church, encouraging and strengthening them. That's the power of prayer and a simple example of one expression of it in a working environment. Of all the essential ingredients for work, prayer at work has to be at the heart. It has, countless times, been the key that opened or closed situations in my own experience.

Disciples of prayer at work

Isaac Newton said, 'All my discoveries have been made in answer to prayer.' Prayer is one of the most underrated, under-marketed, under-explored elements in the life of Christians at work today. Our approach to it individually, and as a church, can be so stereotyped, so predictable and so utterly unimaginative.

The New Testament resonates with prayer. There are more references to prayer than there are to the kingdom of God. We know we're commanded to 'seek first the kingdom', and yet of equal weight are the examples and injunctive to pray. We can't find the kingdom of God without prayer.

Prayer was central for Jesus' life. The fact is that prayer preceded all he did and prayer followed all he did.

Jesus did not pray out of obligation or obedience – he prayed because it was natural to him and he prayed because he loved to communicate with his Father more than anything else. He knew that his own spiritual resources needed topping up from time-to-time. How often do we assume something that Jesus never assumed. We can assume that we have the grace and strength to handle what God gives us to handle – but we don't if we won't pray!

Just because God opens doors of work opportunity or ministry, or both, we cannot assume that all will go well automatically. Everything God gives us to do is intended to be done in genuine partnership with the Holy Spirit. That partnership can only be activated, or realised, by the process of prayer.

Someone once asked Dwight Moody, the famous evangelist, 'Have you been filled with the Holy Spirit?' 'Yes,' he replied, 'but I leak!' We need to believe this and understand its relevance and it will help us substantially to become disciples capable of living with the struggles of daily life. When we give out relationally or spiritually at work, we don't automatically get topped up – we need to go back to prayer for God's refill.

An air conditioner needs to be constantly topped up with water, but the reservoir is usually hidden. Because it's hidden, you can't always easily tell that it's empty. It will run for a while, start to give out unwanted heat and then finally burn out. It can so often be like that for working men and women. If anyone on this planet could have managed without prayer, it was Jesus himself. And yet Jesus made it clear time after time that he was unable to do anything in his own authority. In John's Gospel,

Jesus says, 'I speak just what the Father has taught me', 'I stand with the Father who sent me', 'These words you hear are not my own, they belong to the Father who sent me', 'I can only do what I see the Father doing', 'By myself I can do nothing. I judge only as I hear'.

How did Jesus see what the Father was doing? How did he hear what the Father was saying? How did he know when the Father was sending him? How did he get taught by the Father? The answer is prayer. It was in the process of prayer that Jesus drew his vision, healing, understanding and certainty about timing. Surely we kid ourselves if we think we can find it anywhere else.

When our kids were young, we used to love playing hide and seek. I remember one of the kids saying, 'I'll go and hide and if you can't find me, I'll be in the airing cupboard.' Playing hide and seek is a fun game, even if you do get a bit of a lead. But I bet you didn't know that God invented the game – just take a look in Proverbs: 'It's the glory of God to hide . . . it is the glory of kings to search . . .'

The disciples and the crowds regularly hunted and searched for Jesus, like some divine game of hide and seek. The funny thing was, they nearly always found him in the same place. He still plays the game and I can tell you where to find him – I know where he hides! Would you like to know where he hides? I'll tell you. The crowds and the disciples found him – in the place of prayer.

Nothing has changed. You and I can find Jesus in exactly the same place – the place of prayer. Jesus Christ, the same yesterday, today and forever.

Augustus Strong said, 'The impulse to prayer within our hearts is evidence that Christ is urging our claims in Heaven.' J. Elliot said, 'God is still on the throne, we are still on his footstool and there is only a knee's distance between them!' If we want to know what the Father says in the machine shop, in the school, in the office, on the ward or in our software department, then we will find that in the place of prayer.

Sometimes such talk brings heaviness, or a sense of failure – I just can't pray like that. There is one easy way any of us can do it. I am often reminded of this by the hot-air balloons that frequently fly over our home in Hampshire. You look at them and think to yourself, 'they are going to crash land, they are getting too low'. Then as you watch you hear this huge roar of gas as the pilot lights the burner, sometimes for seconds, sometimes for a minute or two, and that simple short burst lifts the balloon heavenwards again. All of us can handle short burst prayers, in the shower, on the phone, in the kitchen, driving, at our desks, in the office loo, wherever and whenever we need to or want to. Do that for 2 minutes each time, ten times a day and you have prayed an extra 20 minutes a day. That's just over 2 hours of prayer a week, and everyone of us can do it that way. What's really great is that those short bursts of prayer lift us heavenward again – we're still flying.

An approach to prayer for disciples to follow

Are there any clues from the life of Jesus which can help us with prayer? The answer is – yes, loads! One of the most helpful is a model which Jesus gave, in Matthew's Gospel, which enables us to pray by God-given topics and which give us a powerful framework for our prayer time.

First, let us look at some terms used in the Gospels which give us 'video clips' of Jesus at prayer. Before I share them, let me ask you to visualise your own prayer times. Close your eyes and think about where you pray. Where are you? What is going on around you? What sights and sounds are impacting you?

I wonder what your answer was? My guess is that most of you saw images of your lounge or dining room, your office or kitchen. There is one common problem with every one of those places. Can you guess what it is? In a word, distractions. Invariably, there are jobs crying out to be done, people wanting your time, carpets to hoover or last night's dishes to wash.

If Jesus were standing in front of you now, and you asked him the same question, I think I know exactly what words would come to his mind. The following is a list of the answers he has already given to that question.

Images of Jesus at prayer

Often
Withdrew
Secret
Shut the door of your room
Lonely places and prayed
Went out
To a mountainside
Spent the night praying to God
Facial appearance changed
As usual
Reaching the place
He said 'pray'
Privately
Solitary place
On a mountainside
By himself to pray
When evening came
Alone
Very early in the morning
While it was still dark
Got up
Left house
Went off to solitary place

I am touched – moved – when I read these descriptions. I wonder what images filled your mind as we read them together. I find it so fascinating that it doesn't tell us much about what he said, but describes in detail when, where and how. This is a great study for us to do at home, but let me pick on a few areas.

He got away, right away. He withdrew – that is an active choice, a discipline, for disciples in a busy world. He had to get away privately to a solitary place. He had to be alone, he had to be 'by himself to pray'. He found lonely places. When did I last withdraw? When did you last find a lonely place to pray privately? The funny thing is, if you are not used to it, you may find some difficulties at first, like fear of the open, of animals, of aloneness or busyness trying to crowd in.

And one of the first lessons you learn is to overcome these things by prayer!

Very early in the morning, while it was still dark, he got up and left the house. Again, Jesus is choosing times when there is no one else around. He leaves the house, with its job lists, its busyness and its people, and he is off on his prayer walk.

Jesus walked and prayed. Ron Trudinger, one of my closest mentors for years, drummed the 'walk and pray' concept into me. I find it so helpful. I am a fairly active, even hyperactive, individual, so it helps me settle my soul and plug in to God – it gets me motoring. I have one friend who walks 7 miles most days, and prays as he goes, and his answers over the years have been quite amazing. Walking and praying can be a sensible option for people in their working environment. It's one way to get some prayer in without raising problems in the process.

Back to Jesus. He gets up in the morning, he gets up in the dark and he goes at sunset in the cool of the evening. He did it often. The Bible says 'as usual'. This was his normal practice, not unusual or abnormal, but usual. 'On reaching the place' – there was one special place, in a garden or on a mountain. That one place was so special, that he faced all the horrors of the cross in the familiar, reassuring sweetness of that usual place.

When we lived in Basingstoke, I had a place – a special place – where I was at home with God. I can remember most of the times I was there very clearly, and it was a place where I saw what the Father was doing and heard what he was saying (it was a small area known as Bedlam Bottom). In Whitchurch, where we now live, I have a fabulous place overlooking Watership Down – it has been my 'usual' place, my lonely place.

Several times, Jesus was recorded as praying on the mountainside. A couple of times a year I try to get away, for example into the Pennines, and when I am there one of the things I love to do is to walk into the hills. Every time I have done it, Jesus has met me.

A stone's throw

In the hour of his greatest anguish, Jesus went to the one place where he knew he could meet with his Father. This is how Mark

describes it: 'Jesus went out as usual to the Mount of Olives . . .
he withdrew about a *stone's throw* beyond them and knelt down
. . . .'

Nearly all Jesus' prayer was solitary, in lonely places, at quiet
times, on mountains. For the average Christian, most of our
prayer takes place in stuffy homes, sitting down, feeling drowsy
and constricted. If we are going to be disciples, let us follow him
into the open, into the lonely places, into the private, into the
'usual place' – our special spot.

The 'usual place' gets associated with prayer and, in the open,
God's creation frees our mind, lifts our spirit and primes our
heart for prayer. My sons, Joshua and Joel, have created a small
area at the furthest point of our garden, about a stone's throw
from the house, where we can go and be alone, build a fire, or
walk around. Some of this book was written down there. The
beauty of 'the stone's throw' is that it is just far enough to still be
near your closest friends, but far enough away to be out of
earshot and distractions. If you work in a busy city office, you can
find a stone's throw near a small fountain area, grassed area,
parkland or whatever. I remember one particularly stressful period in my life, I would take a 10-minute coffee break or 15 minutes
at lunch and walk into a small area of woodland adjacent to our
town-based office block. Those stone's throw moments were a
salvation.

15.

Discipling in the World of Work

This was not one of the best days of my life. I had been running some businesses for the church. We had set up one of the largest Christian bookshops in the country and we were also running a publishing house and a growing printing press. At the time we were exploring the role of church in business and we very quickly discovered the practical and biblical wisdom that the church elders have no place running a business as part of their elders' role. I had contributed to the discussion and the decision, but it was painful. The printing press was sold to another company, and as part of the arrangement I was going with it!

Today was my first day at the new venture and I was feeling very low. The feeling of leaving the church's employ was a bit shattering and the future was one big 'unknown' ahead of me. Brian Rebbettes was my new boss, and he and his wife took me out for a picnic lunch at the Aldermaston woods close by. As we sat there that first day, chatting away, their loving act coupled with an encouraging card from Gill, my wife, began to give me hope, and more than that, it began to posture me towards something new.

What followed in the subsequent years were some of the most formative experiences in my life. Brian began to disciple me at work. He looked for ways to open doors of function for me and ways to sharpen my selling skills. He shared his office with me so that I could listen to him on the phone. We could congratulate each other on successes and discuss the failures. He was the first and only man to really confront me on my love of money. He challenged me in my marriage and encouraged me with my children. We would share scriptures and revelation together, and we often prayed together.

Brian put his money and support into ideas that I created and actually participated in those new ideas himself. When he sensed I had something worthwhile to say, he would find church groups for me to share with. He and his wife, Anne, taught Gill and I to have weekends away, and their generosity made them possible. Here was a man who called me up to be what God had made me to be. Here was a man who lived the kingdom of God at work. Here was a man who served God in his business, who loved God and loved his staff and who, in the process, discipled many of them. When Brian ultimately sold his business and we both moved on to different things, I actually felt bereaved and the feeling of loss was with me for many years afterwards. What an example, what a privilege to be mentored in that way and what a responsibility to live up to!

Discipling at work

The working world is desperate for practical solutions to life dilemmas, not just work dilemmas. The training world today freely uses the term 'mentoring' and 'coaching'. It is not even rare – it is common and accepted practice. The chances are, if you are a nurse or a teacher, a manager or a lathe operator, you have already experienced mentoring or coaching.

In the last 20 years or so, thousands of you reading this book have been trained and discipled in your churches, and you carry a treasure that God may well want you to invest in helping others.

Gerry was a non-Christian who worked for one of my UK clients. 'David,' he said. 'Would you consider mentoring me? I don't know what it means, but I would really appreciate it.' My response was, 'Let me think about it.' When I had reflected, I came back and this is what I said, 'Gerry, you know my faith. If I mentor you, it will be inevitable that I weave my faith into the experience, because that is who I am, and it is an integral part of my own development.' Gerry didn't hesitate. 'I expected that,' he said. 'Shall we go for it?'

We had some wonderful times, usually an extended lunchtime with my client's blessing, once a month. Each month, I gave

Gerry an assignment. The last one was to find ten things that he could learn from in the life of Jesus and his leadership. When we met next, we had some pressing business and my intention was to leave it for the next month. I could sense that somehow this was really important to Gerry. He was almost insistent that we discuss it. Gerry began to read the ten things. He got to point three or four and he started to shake, he found it hard to get the words out. What were those words? Let me quote them for you, 'Come unto me all you who are weary and heavy laden and I will give you rest. Take my yoke upon you and learn of me, for my yoke is easy and my burden is light.'

What was going on? It's simple – Gerry had been asking some questions of me in the mentoring process, and he was getting his answers direct from God's Word. Those words answered some questions for Gerry and, among other things, enabled him to see that a change of role was a desirable next step. Gerry moved on but we keep in contact, and in fact we met up recently. He has been through Alpha and given his life to God.

I had a client in the USA – someone I respect highly and who in fact has mentored me over the years without realising it. He asked me to quote for coaching one of his senior sales staff. When we had agreed the contract, he said, 'David, I believe this concept is good, but there is going to be real value in you giving some of your personal mentoring or discipling for this man, and that is what I am really excited about.'

I relate these two examples because it is not my natural 'forte'. I don't often offer coaching or mentoring in my business arena. I am not even particularly good at discipling in the church world. I mention these examples because, if God can do it through me, he can surely do it – and probably better – through you.

I suppose I would love to provoke and challenge you – you almost certainly have more under the bonnet than you realise. Could it be that there are people in your office, your shop floor, your ward, your practice or among your clients, who have been asking for mentoring without using the word? Could it be with a bit of prayer and alertness you could be 'God's answer with skin on' to a colleague, a peer or even a manager. Who knows?

Let me give you another example from my friend Chris Lever:

Over a 4-year period, we had been working with a European headquarters group of senior managers. We had become close to them, with the relationship shifting from consultant to trusted friend. A corporate buy-out had suddenly left them without jobs. What had once been a team full of sparkle, energy and a 'can do' mentality was quickly reduced to a group without hope. Individuals had put their life and their very soul into building their part of the business. For many, it had cost them a lot, but they had paid the price because they figured what they were trying to create was worth it. What took years to build was suddenly disassembled overnight. As they faced the future, with questions like, 'So, what has the last 10 years been about?', 'Have I got what it takes to go on?', 'Do I have the courage to start something new?', 'I didn't realise I would feel like this – who can I trust now?' we shared a few tears, because we shared their pain. You see, we had walked with them on their journey. We told our story, one which has seen great blessing and great pain, too. We shared the dilemmas that we had faced and we shared our hope. Together, we explored in depth their hopes and fears and where confidence was located. Over some months, we saw a shift in thinking, attitude and desire. Hope had begun to return. We had the tremendous privilege of hearing and exploring people's dreams and of standing with them as each made hard choices. We served them as best we could. A year on, we are thrilled to see many of the 'half-baked' ideas we had shared together being realised. They say that we inspired their dreams. I think all we did was listen, care and breathe some hope into weary souls.

Chris goes on to say,

My sadness, is that in all the years I have been a Christian too many have not experienced real coaching from those in leadership of their church groups. We have certainly been talked at, taught endlessly on subjects which have fascinated the teachers but have often lacked real-world relevance. But all of this misses the point. Coaching is a practical, applicable and transferable process which seeks to make a difference. You see God has great and audacious plans for each one of us. There is work for all of us to do in our own unique way and context and he wants us to be successful. To complete the work he has given each one of us to do, we will need to learn, and learning isn't just about filling our heads with knowledge. It is a much more dynamic and fun process than that.

Let me describe two men who were, for me, coaches of the highest order. Neither were Christians but were exemplars and master coaches that we in the church can learn from if we have the humility to do so.

Martin Underwood was an England rugby international who on retirement went on to write about and coach rugby. While studying at St. Luke's, Exeter, I had the great privilege of being coached by Martin. I remember those sessions as if they were yesterday. He got me to do things that were beyond anything I dreamed I could do. He was inspiring by voice and example, he showed you what he wanted, and we practised time and time again to get it right. When we got it wrong, because we hadn't mastered some finer point, he patiently explained and encouraged us, watching us perform and celebrating with us when it did work. When we got it wrong because we weren't trying, he bawled us out and I can still remember that gut-wrenching feeling of letting him and ourselves down. But he would never let you stay in that place. He would get you up and moving and he would then fall into a stream of encouragement. In his great company, it was me that felt important. What was more, I was just a very, very ordinary player surrounded by stars, but he always treated each one of us just the same because his mission was to help each player be all that he could be, and then just a little bit more.

And then there is my good friend Bob Hale. Bob was born into a fishing family and went on to become a master shipwright. Over several years, almost single-handedly he built his first passenger vessel. The effort almost killed him.

I am the son of a marine commando and was brought up in and around the docks and ships, and the sea has remained a deep love. It has been my soul food. When I was a kid, I turned up on quayside looking for a job on a passenger ferry. Bob was the first person I approached and without an interview (that I recognised) he gave me a job as deckhand. On my first day I was in heaven; I had all of the dirty jobs to do but he made me understand that on ship everything needs to be spot on. So cleaning the brass work on the wheel took on real meaning and importance. And on that first day after we had finished our work, he took us out to sea and let me drive the vessel home with him standing at my side. From that day on, he was always showing me how to do things, always letting me practise. I can only wonder now at how he must have felt when standing at my side he let me berth the *Water Gypsy* for the first time. And we learnt together – I learnt to give him space and he was always asking me questions about what I thought about this and that. His patience was endless. When I became first mate and was on the wheel, he would stand in front of me, motioning with his hand which way and how far he wanted me to turn. Nothing was ever done in a hurry and he never wrenched the wheel away from me even when I was off line. He became a close friend and we confided in each other and had adventures together. Always by my side, he helped me prepare for my skipper's licence, asking me questions and practising manoeuvres and routines. He also used to take me to obscure wood yards searching for the exact bit of oak that was to finish off his new vessel he was having built. All the time he was teaching me and instilling in me a love of material and a deep understanding of the job it was to do. When I did get my skipper's licence, he gave me the *Water Gypsy* as my first command. The gift could not have been greater because I know how much of himself was in that beautiful boat. He charged me just one thing to do, and that was to bring on others in my crew, seeing beyond their rough edges into their potential. And I have been trying to do that ever since.

Two great coaches, very different to each other but both have made a difference to me. Both were in it for just that reason.

When Jesus called the disciples, I wonder what he saw. And I wonder what I would have seen. Whether he saw what they would become in his church or whether he merely glimpsed the possibility of what might be, I can't say, but he did see something beyond the sweat-stained, rough-looking fishermen that everyone knew.

I long for the time when our leaders see beyond just the few stars who might lead the church and be the next 'big names', to the ordinary businessmen and women, to the teachers and health workers, to the gardeners and window cleaners and to the house parents who opt to stay at home with their new families. I hope, too, that they get the message that their role is about equipping and releasing people to their work.

For such a time as this

Our fractured world and our work colleagues, with their fractured relationships and fractured dreams, need mending. Could it be that 'for such a time as this' God has placed you in your workplace? I believe that the world of work is ready to hear some good news. *So love work, live life and go and make disciples.* How about it?

16.

How to Eat This Elephant

I hope this book has been a motivating, challenging and impacting read. But please don't put it down here. The time you have invested in reading it could transform your life, your church, your family and your destiny.

But of course it never will! It is destined to fail, destined to be a disappointment. Why? Because you won't apply it, will you? Come on now, be honest, you are about to put this book away, aren't you? You told yourself that you would try to apply some of these principles when you next get a chance. Don't kid yourself! Do something now, and there is a chance that you will make a difference. Leave it, and you never will.

How do you eat this elephant? Easy, the same way you eat any elephant – one bite at a time. Take this material, ask God what needs re-reading, what needs changing and in your prayer diary, or in a chat to a colleague, commit yourself to enact that change.

If you feel excited about the thought of starting your own business have a read of Appendix I. If you are a church leader, would you go to Appendix III and fill in the action form? If you want to fax or email us with your commitment, feel free. If you are in the workplace and you feel challenged to do something in your home church, please read Appendix II and fill in your personal action plan.

A favour!

Write down the five key truths or ideas that you know intuitively will give you the greatest change immediately and which God has spoken to you as you have read this book. Jot them down in the space below.

1 _____

Action: _____

2 _____

Action: _____

3 _____

Action: _____

4 _____

Action _____

5 _____

Action: _____

Please use these at the next possible opportunity. Promise me this: if they work for you, write down the next five and try them. That is the 10 per cent rule. Take just 10 per cent of the areas you know need to change and focus on them. When you have mastered them, go on to the next 10 per cent and so on. Keep doing it and you will not only read but begin to implement your work as a place of destiny.

God bless you as you put these principles into practice.

RESOURCES FROM DAVID OLIVER

Audio CDs
Four hours of David Oliver (live) delivering this material on audio CD for just £10.
For details email enquiries@insight-marketing.com

Workplace Resources
Care for the Family have a range of workplace resources including:

The Heart of Success, Rob Parson's bestselling book.
Beating Stress and Burnout, a video resource with workbooks.
The Heart of Success study guide and workbooks.
Love Work, Live Life! study guide and workbooks.

For a full list of resources email enquiries@letsdolife.com

Business Resources
To receive David's FREE Monthly Business E-newsletter please email davido@insight-marketing.com or call 0870 787 7404

Training
David Oliver has trained well in excess of 100,000 people worldwide and specialises in in-house training and keynote delivery in:
Negotiation
Sales
Strategic Customer Care
Closing More Sales
Gaining High Value Clients Through Innovative Marketing
Leadership

For more details email davido@insight-marketing.com or call 0870 7877404

For a list of audio training resources on CD please visit www.insight-marketing.com

Outsourced Marketing Functions
For information on outsourced lead generation and marketing clinics please visit www.insight-marketing.com

Amazing Family, Church or Corporate Experiences on a Yacht
For family or corporate packages on a 36-foot yacht please visit www.yachtsforfun.com

Love Work, Live Life! and Care for the Family – National Events
Care for the Family run regular workplace events. For full details of their national evening programmes and their sector specific national events call 029 2081 0800 or visit www.careforthefamily.org.uk and look for events

Keynote Talks
If you are interested in having a keynote speech for your business on a range of topics including:
    Leaders or managers – which should we be and why?
    Work life balance for improved profitability
    Stress and learning the difference between the clock and the
      compass
    Marketing
    Sales skills
    Negotiation

Call 0870 787 7404 or email enquiries@insight-marketing.com

Churches
If you are interested in organising a one-day event with David Oliver please call to discuss.

Insight Marketing
Cricket Corner
Lynch Hill Park
Whitchurch
RG28 7NF
Tel: 0870 787 7404
Fax: 0870 787 7405
Email: davido@insight_marketing.com

USEFUL SCRIPTURES

Chapter 1: Luke 11:51, Genesis 4:2–4, Mark 6:3, Acts 9:43, Acts 18:18–26, 1 Corinthians 16:19, Acts 16:14.

Chapter 2: Ephesians 2:10, Psalm 139:13–16.

Chapter 4: Psalm 139:13–16, 1 Corinthians 2:9, Luke 17:21, Philippians 3:12, 1 Chronicles 20:20.

Chapter 5: Ephesians 1:18, 2:10, 3:8–21, 4:18–23, 5:23–30, Matthew 7:15, 16:16–19, 1 Timothy 3:15, Acts 2:47, 6:12, 14:22–23, 20:21, 20:28.

Chapter 6: Corinthians 14:1–28, Ephesians 3:16, Mark 6:3, Exodus 31:3, Ecclesiastes 10:10, Matthew 25:30.

Chapter 8: 1 Thessalonians 5:21, Romans 13:6, Revelation 2:7.

Chapter 9: 1 Chronicles 31:20–21, James 1:7–8, Proverbs 30:18–19, 1 Thessalonians 5:18, Luke 3:14, Hebrews 13:5, Ephesians 4:2–8, Proverbs 26:10.

Chapter 10: Isaiah 43:1, Genesis 32:28, James 1:2–4, Hebrews 5:8, Hebrews 4:15, Mark 6:3, Proverbs 1:20–23, Revelation 2:26–29, Deuteronomy 28:13, Daniel 6:1–3, Titus 1:5–9, 1 Timothy 3:1–13, 1 Timothy 6:1, 1 Peter 2:12–18, Hebrews 10:38, Romans 4:12, Galatians 5:25, Romans 14:23, Hebrews 11:6, 2 Corinthians 1:24, Romans 10:9.

Chapter 11: James 5:16, Luke 16:13, Deuteronomy 14:29, 15:10, 16:15, 24:19, 28:1–14, 30:9, Proverbs 11:12, 13:11, 13:21–22, 20:21, 21:17, 21:23, 24:29, Psalm 34:9, 35:27, 37:37, James 4:3, Ecclesiastes 5:19, Luke 14:33, Luke 18:22.

Chapter 12: Acts 1:8, 2 Chronicles 31:21, Ecclesiastes 9:10, Colossians 3:23, Matthew 9:29, Romans 12:6, Hebrews 13:5, Galatians 6:9, 1 John 3:18, Acts 2:17–21, Joel 2:28–32, 1 Timothy 1:18–19.

Chapter 13: Proverbs 25:2, Matthew 6, Hebrews 7:25, 1 Samuel 1:15, Psalm 42:4, Psalm 62:8, Philippians 4:6, 1 Thessalonians 5:17.

Chapter 14: Matthew 11:30, 28:19.

BIBLIOGRAPHY

Chapter 1
Dennis Peacocke, *Almighty and Sons*, Sovereign World Books.

Chapter 2
George MacDonald, *The Curate's Awakening*, Bethany House Publishing.

Chapter 3
Os Guinness, *The Call*, Authentic.
Rob Parsons, *The Heart of Success*, Hodder & Stoughton.

Chapter 6
George MacDonald, *The Curate's Awakening*, Bethany House Publishing.
Peter Wagner, *Your Spiritual Gifts Can Help Your Church Grow*, Regal Books.

Chapter 7
Charles Kingsley, *Life Letters*, out of print.
Ralph L. Lewis and Gregg Lewis, *Learning To Preach Like Jesus*, Crossway Books.
Derek Kinder, *Proverbs* (page 24), IVP.

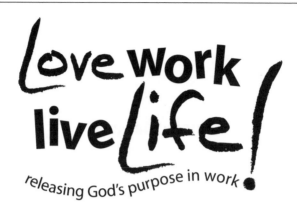

Love Work live Life!

releasing God's purpose in work

Work   what's it all about?

The **Love Work, Live Life!** initiative from Care for the Family approaches the issues and challenges of work from a uniquely Christian perspective.

Through regional events and national conferences, you'll discover what the Bible *really* says about work and how God seeks to work alongside every Christian in whatever work they do.

Love Work, Live Life! is presented by businessman and popular speaker David Oliver, and shatters the myth that the only work God is interested in is full time Christian service.

"David's down to earth message of hope and encouragement can spark a new love for your work making a difference to every one of us."

Rob Parsons, Executive Director, Care for the Family

For further details, visit **www.lovework.org.uk** or call **(029) 2081 0800** to find out where the nearest **Love Work, Live Life!** event is to you!

care FOR THE family